"They Call Me Naughty Lola"

Personal Ads from
the *London Review of Books*

Edited and with an
Introduction by David Rose

SCRIBNER

New York London Toronto Sydney

SCRIBNER
1230 Avenue of the Americas
New York, NY 10020

First Scribner edition 2006
Originally published in Great Britain in 2006 by Profile Books UK
Published by arrangement with Profile Books UK

SCRIBNER and design are trademarks of Macmillan Library
Reference USA, Inc., used under license by Simon & Schuster,
the publisher of this work.

For information regarding special discounts for bulk purchases,
please contact Simon & Schuster Special Sales at 1-800-465-6798
or business@simonandschuster.com
Designed by Sue Lamble
Set in Quadraat
Manufactured in the United States of America

10 9 8 7 6 5 4 3 2 1

Library of Congress Cataloging-in-Publication Data is available.

ISBN 978-1-4165-4030-4

This book is dedicated to Molly Parkin,
Jamie Carragher, Evel Knievel and Nicola.

Contents

“They Call Me
Naughty Lola”

Introduction

The *London Review of Books* personal ads began in
October 1998, with the simple idea of helping people
with similar literary and cultural tastes get together.
We hoped the column might be a sort of *84 Charing
Cross Road* endeavour, with readers providing their
own versions of Anthony Hopkins and Anne Bancroft
finding love among the bookshelves. The first ad
we received was from a man 'on the look-out for a
contortionist who plays the trumpet'.

In truth, there are few people who can adequately
summarise themselves in the thirty or so words that
make up the average lonely-heart ad. There are few
products or concepts that can be summarised in the
same space, so it's unreasonable to assume that a
description of all the complexities and subtleties that
make up a person can be trimmed down to a couple
of abstract sentences. Add to this the many inherent
psychological issues at stake in the placing of a lonely
heart – guilt, nervousness, fear of rejection – and
an ad can be an accident waiting to happen or an
anticlimactic event that fizzles out into an episode of
one's life best forgotten.

Because of the dangers of looking slightly foolish,
and because of the difficulties of being concise when
talking about ourselves, lonely hearts ads, appearing

in many publications throughout the world usually become fairly homogenous statements that often default to bland physical descriptions. Height, weight, eye and hair colour are all standard, but so too is every clichéd adjective that can be applied to them. Eyes will be 'dazzling', 'bright', 'seductive', but little else. Advertisers will be 'slender' or 'cuddly', possibly 'flame-haired', or all too often inappropriately compared to a celebrity – 'looks a bit like George Clooney'. The main factor in the success of garnering responses with this type of ad is the wishful thinking of the reader, who will fashion an image of the advertiser based on what little information has been given together with what it is they've been looking for all these years. The first exchange of photographs, therefore, will often prove disappointing when it's realised that the advertiser isn't Angelina Jolie but an arthritic old sailor with scalp problems.

There are notable exceptions. The *New York Review of Books* has a remarkably successful lonely-hearts section, and the demographic of readers is quite similar to that of the LRB – middle-class, well-educated, intellectual. Rather than list physical attributes, typically advertisers in the NYRB pitch incredibly positive aspects of their personality. They use their thirty-odd words to talk about things they like: favourite seasons, favourite authors, beaches they're fond of or lakeside walks they enjoy. As a model of lonely hearts it is very encouraging, if at times a little starchy.

The advertisers in the *London Review of Books*, however, are rarely inhibited by positive thinking and they don't tend to suffer the same degree of nervous overstatement found in other lonely-hearts sections. They have pitched themselves variously over the years as 'bald and irascible' or 'dour and uninteresting' or 'hostile and high-maintenance'. Such a self-denigrating and all too honest approach carries a distinctive note of charm. It's hard, for example, not to fall instantly in love with

I'd like to dedicate this advert to my mother (difficult cow, 65) who is responsible for me still being single at 36. Man. 36. Single. Held at home by years of subtle emotional abuse and at least 19 fake heart-attacks. Box no. 6207.

Monday mornings are a regular harvest time for personal ads. In the natural order of things they follow the lonely heart's weekend of solitary wine-drinking in front of *Taggart* on UK Gold. Consequently, the ads in my post-weekend email inbox tend to have more of a hangover about them than others, or the smoky whiff of a solipsistic Saturday night still in full melancholic tilt and hanging heavy in the adjectives. The authors are 'unbeaten', 'down but not out', 'fighters' or 'terminally disappointed'. By mid-week the ads are much less gin-soaked in tone and much less likely to mention the advertiser's preferences for adopting naval ranks in the bedroom. Personally I prefer the weekenders. Apart from anything else they're much chattier when I have to call to say they've given the Ceefax recipe page instead of a valid credit-card number.

People who place small ads are rarely salesmen or advertising creatives. So they often fail to meet the basic principles of advertising. Typically, an ad for, say, a BMW car or a Prada shoe or an insurance scheme has less than half a second to attract the attention of a magazine browser, amid pages of stiff competition. This is far more difficult for a lonely heart who doesn't have the resources or expertise to produce a glossy, full-page ad brimming with clever copy and zippy graphics. But if a personal ad manages in its few words to hold the gaze of the reader a little while longer than its competitors, then it's a long way down the road to getting a reply. And seizing attention to provoke a reply, rather than actually finding a mate, is initially the point of all personal ads.

The Russian critical theorist Viktor Shklovsky identified the processes of arresting a reader's attention, citing phrases, motifs or concepts that seem incongruous within a surrounding text.[1] He used the term *ostranenie*, or defamiliarisation – literally 'making strange'. It's tempting to venture that advertisers in the LRB personal ads adhere to these early Russian Formalist principles. The casual reader would expect the standard formula of 'Man, leonine looks, 5′ 11″, regularly works out, enjoys cinema'. Instead they'd get this:

On 15 March 1957, Commander J. R. Hunt of the United States Navy landed at Key West Florida in his non-rigid

1 Viktor Shklovsky, 'Art as Technique' in *Russian Formalist Criticism: Four Essays*, translated and edited by Lee T. Lemon and Marion J. Reis (University of Nebraska Press, 1965), pp. 5–24.

airship having travelled for 264 hours and 12 minutes without once refuelling. Coincidentally, that's the same length of time as I've spent without once making contact with a woman (apart from my mother, who doesn't count, but who only ever asks me what I'd like for breakfast – it's eggs; I like eggs for breakfast, poached, please, on two slices of granary bread). Is this a world record? Answers, please, to 37-year-old male idiot. Box no. 2169.

If *ostranenie* is their strategy, they are shrewd advertisers indeed and this possibly gives the ads more credit than is strictly warranted. None the less it's all too easy to underestimate the discursive gymnastics behind

More than just a personal ad! This is your ticket to a world of pleasure. Write now to Putney care assistant and weekend league bowler (48). Box no. 7721.

A lonely heart also provides clues and hints for the reader to interpret. The response to each ad depends as much on what can be inferred as on what is explicitly stated, which is often as little as the advertiser's gender and geographic location. In its remaining few words and phrases the ad has to convey a sense of the author's personality; the inferences of the reader are crucial. What is it we can infer from, for example, 'Man, 34, Worcs., WLTM F to 35 with the sort of attributes that make the NetNanny my mother installed on my PC go off like a 1978 Ford Capri discharging up a dinosaur's rectum'? There's a PhD's worth of material to be gathered from this ad alone, and at least a year's employment for any newly qualified social worker.

While many LRB personals are similarly off-beat they're not without their share of responses. It doesn't claim to be the most successful lonely-hearts column in the world (far from it) but it has given rise to friendships, marriages, at least one birth, and at least one divorce after a marriage resulting from an ad in it. There are also plenty of advertisers ready to call in to complain about getting no responses whatsoever despite the LRB enjoying a readership known in marketing circles to be more responsive than most. This isn't so surprising – whatever the responsiveness of the readership, the advertiser still has to do a bit of work. You can lead a horse to water, but you can't make it avoid talking about its mother or cats:

Coming from one of the world's largest coal-producing regions, you'd expect me to litter this ad with clever references to coal and the decline of the coal industry and possibly some nostalgia about my father working in a coal mine and a few anecdotes about accidents and heroism and camaraderie and everyone supporting each other in times of coal-related hardship and crisis. Instead, I'd like to talk about my cats. Gentleman, 55. Likes cats. Box no. 5380.

Advertising for a lover or a soul mate or a marriage partner has always existed in some form or other. But the protocols of advertising in lonely hearts have changed considerably over the years. Lonely hearts from the nineteenth century show men specifying their annual incomes rather than giving any hint of

physical appearance; today this would be deemed
crude. Nowadays it's also considered coarse to be
exact about age; women, in particular, are discouraged
from stating how old they are, and are advised instead
to give the age range of the partner they're seeking.
Advertisers in the LRB, however, have no truck with
such conventions and will often specify the income
required of any prospective partner, their own
level of personal debt and their age to the exact day
(occasionally in dog years), along with weight, slipper
size and favourite type of soup:

What's your favourite soup? Mine is mulligatawny.
Mulligatawny-liking gentleman (50). Box no. 4401.

Some rudimentary statistical analysis is possible.
Whereas women tend to supply the majority of
personal ads in other publications, the split is fairly
even in the LRB (49 per cent women, 51 per cent men)
and the age range reflects that of the readers of the
magazine, between thirty-five and fifty-five. Women
who specify their employment are likely to work in
publicity departments (28 per cent of all named female
occupations). Men who cite their occupation are often
lecturers (35 per cent of all named male occupations
– 71 per cent of them in the fields of classics and
history). There have been plenty of scientists, far too
many poets and, encouragingly for an increasingly
mechanised society, at least two stevedores. Seven per
cent of women applying adjectives describe themselves
as 'edgy' or 'highly strung' (these account for 83 per
cent of those working in publicity departments), while

8 per cent of men mention their mother and 2 per cent enjoy the music of Bachman-Turner Overdrive (of which 63 per cent are forty-two-year-old classics lecturers still living at home with their mum). In the early months of the LRB personal column, women and men were equally likely to ask for respondents who were 'intelligent', 'thoughtful' or 'well read'. These days the men are much happier to receive a full medical prescription history rather than a photograph, and the women have long since learned to lower the bar:

Hi. I'm am intelligent, attractive, cultured, recently divorced woman in her early forties looking for a man whose maxim in life isn't 'pull my finger' or 'smelt it, dealt it'. Box no. 5022.

In many publications, help is at hand to guide advertisers through the processes and pitfalls of copywriting so as to avoid any devastating *faux pas*. A lot of newspapers and magazines contract out their lonely-hearts column to agencies that help pen the adverts. Some have simple personality tests and will formulate copy for the advertiser on the basis of the results. The aim is to maximise the number of responses by making sure the advertiser doesn't blow it by mentioning his compulsive gaming habits or her aversion to the colour red or a mishap they had with rabbits during a school trip to Morecambe in 1965. This seems a shame. Every publication has its own particular tone and flavour, and there are only two places where readers can effectively contribute to this:

the letters page and the classified section. A lonely-hearts section is a column of reader contributions more than it is an advertising asset, and it's a mistake to homogenise it for the sake of additional revenue. There is a currency in lonely hearts that goes beyond mere numbers.

Moreover, for the brave and the bold, there is a lot of fun to be had in the process of finding a mate, be it through dating agencies or singles nights or lonely-hearts ads. Indeed for some LRB advertisers meeting a partner is no longer even the main objective of placing a personal ad. Creating these silly little flourishes has become an art form, successfully side-stepping the potentially awkward self-appraisal of other lonely-hearts columns. They're a frolic, a bit of whimsy. If they earn responses, then so much the better, but the stakes aren't high if they don't. The silliness, in this sense, becomes a sleight of hand, a trick done with mirrors to disguise the machinery beneath the stage:

Writing this advert has given the biggest sense of accomplishment I've felt since successfully ironing my trousers (14 June 1998). Man, 37. Box no. 2473.

Having fun is an important element in breaking down the anxieties that have made us so acutely hopeless when it comes to speaking about relationships, and I like to think the LRB personals have played their small part. Pitching oneself in the LRB is no longer about trying to locate one's most attractive aspects, principally because it's tiring trying to figure out what other people find attractive. The ads in the LRB aren't necessarily about saying anything at all; they are little statements of absurdity – flashes of silliness that brilliantly, if briefly, illuminate the human condition and all its attendant quirks and nonsenses.

There have been many Monday mornings when, opening those emails that have accumulated during the small hours of the weekend, I've clutched my head in despair and wept like a little child, wishing they could be more straightforward or at least toy with the idea of being conventional. But more often than not I'm glad of their eccentricity. I'm grateful for the 'Low-carbing, high-maintenance F (43)' seeking an M to 50 'with no small knowledge of hiding trigger foods, the protein count of devilled eggs, and nature's own cures for constipation'. It helps me appreciate the importance of silliness and, among other things, the value of a regular bowel movement.

LRB personals exist because of the many hundreds of readers who have contributed so indefatigably to the column over the last decade, and I'm profoundly grateful to them all. Nor should the work of staff at the LRB be underestimated; I'd like to thank Mary-Kay Wilmers and all the editorial and business staff of the LRB for nurturing such a dedicated readership. In particular I'd like to thank the following, without whom this book, and the column itself, would simply have never existed: Tahmina Begum, Howard Bromelow, Ben Campbell, Daniel Crewe, Bryony Dalefield, Penny Daniel, Tim Johnson, Thomas Jones, Daniel Soar, Sara Tsiringakis and Nicholas Spice, who has been a friend and a mentor throughout.

Note to readers: It should be pointed out that the ads in this volume are no longer active and as such responses cannot be forwarded on to advertisers.

**❝Love is strange
— wait 'til you
see my feet❞**

This ad may not be the best lonely heart in the world, nor its author the best-smelling. That's all I have to say. Man, 37. Box no. 7654.

 My finger on the pulse of culture, my ear to the ground of philosophy, my hip in the medical waste bin of Glasgow Royal Infirmary. 14% plastic and counting – geriatric brainiac and compulsive NHS malingering fool (M, 81), looking for richer, older sex-starved woman on the brink of death to exploit and ruin every replacement operation I've had since 1974. Box no. 7648 (quickly, the clock's ticking, and so is this pacemaker).

 7 million is good for me. Most days though I plateau at around 3 million. Any advances? Man with low sperm count (35 – that's my age) seeks woman in no hurry to see the zygotes divide.[1] Box no. 8385.

 Dinner's on me. Gap-toothed F, 32. WLTM man to 35 with permanent supply of Wet Ones. Box no. 7364.

 Remember when all this was open fields, and you could go out and leave your door unlocked? Woman, 24. Inherited her mother's unreasonable and utterly unfounded nostalgia (and her father's hirsute back). WLTM barber with fondness for Sherbet Dib-Dabs and Parma Violets.[2] Box no. 8486.

---

1 A normal average sperm count is 20 million.

2 Sherbet Dib-Dab: square lollipop in a small packet of sherbet, usually licked and dipped. Parma Violet: traditional perfumed violet candy.

Virtually complete male, 63, seeks woman with spares and shed. Box no. 7923.

 Sinister-looking man with a face that only a mother would love: think of an ageing Portillo with a beard and you have my better-looking twin. Sweetie at heart, though. Nice conversation, great for dimly-lit romantic meals. Better in those Welsh villages where the electricity supply can't be guaranteed. Charitable women to 50 appreciated. Box no. 0364.

 Bald, short, fat and ugly male, 53, seeks short-sighted woman with tremendous sexual appetite. Box no. 9612.

 You think I like dressing this way? Lanolin-sensitive Cumbrian chick: outside all calico, inside pure wool. WLTM man to 40 who knows when to turn the lights down and the heat up. First-aid skills a bonus. Box no. 3280.

 I'm just a girl who can't say 'no' (or 'anaesthetist'). Lisping Rodgers and Hammerstein fan, female lecturer in politics (37) WLTM man to 40 for thome enthanted eveningth. Box no. 2498.

 My other car is a bike. Eco-friendly bio-diverse M (29). Smells a bit like soil and eats too much soup, but otherwise friendly (you're not seriously going to put that burger in your mouth, are you?). Box no. 8563.

Love is strange – wait 'til you see my feet. F, 34,
wide-fitting Scholl's.³ Box no. 5973.

You're a brunette, 6', long legs, 25–30, intelligent,
articulate and drop-dead gorgeous. I, on the other
hand, am 4′10″, have the looks of Hervé Villechaize
and carry an odour of wheat.⁴ No returns and no
refunds at box no. 3321.

This personal column has been poorer without me,
so here I am again – hairy-backed Wiltshire troll with
definite *Stig of the Dump* influences (M, 56, jam-jar

---

3   Scholl: shoe-manufacturer specialising in comfort footwear.
Formed in 1904 by Dr William Matthias Scholl. In 1912 Scholl founded
the Illinois College of Chiropody and Orthopaedics.

4   Hervé Jean-Pierre Villechaize. Born 23 April 1943 in Paris, France.
Diagnosed with an acute thyroid condition at the age of three, he
reached a full-grown height of just under four feet tall. Studied
painting and photography at the Beaux-Arts museum in Paris. At the
age of eighteen he became the youngest artist ever to have his work
displayed in the prestigious Museum of Paris. Moved to New York at
the age of twenty-one and became an actor with roles that included
Beppo in *The Gang That Couldn't Shoot Straight* (1971) and Nick Nack
in the 1974 James Bond film *The Man with the Golden Gun*. Failing to
capitalise on these roles, Villechaize eventually found fame playing
the role of Tattoo opposite Ricardo Montalban in ABC's TV show
Fantasy Island, where his catchphrase 'de plane, de plane' entered
the lexicon of American popular culture. Married Donna Camille in
1980; the couple divorced in December 1981. Villechaize was dropped
from *Fantasy Island* in 1983 after demanding more money and fell
into severe financial difficulties. By 1990 his health had deteriorated
and he suffered frequent bouts of depression. In 1993 he found work
in an American Dunkin' Donuts commercial in which he asked for
'de plain, de plain' doughnut. After attending a screening for *The
Fugitive* at the Directors Guild Theater in Hollywood with his partner,
Katherine Self, Villechaize was found on 4 September 1993 with a self-
inflicted gunshot wound in his chest. He was pronounced dead at 3.40
p.m. by doctors at the Medical Center of North Hollywood.

windows, a fridge made of bike parts, and a sensitive grunt during only the most intimate moments), still searching for that special lady with no sense of touch or smell, and a capacity for overwhelming compromise in certain lifestyle choices. Box no. 3732.

 Tonight, female *LRB* readers to 90, I am the hunter and you are my quarry. 117-year-old male Norfolk Viagra bootlegger finally in the mood for a bit of young totty. Which realistically could be any one of you with working hip joints and a minimum 20% lung capacity. Hopeful right through the Complan and Horlicks main course at box no. 3112.

 You were reading the BBC in-house magazine on the Jubilee Line (12 November), I was coughing hot tea through my nostrils. Surely you can't have forgotten? Write now to smitten, weak-kneed, severely burned, bumbling F (32, but normally I look younger). I'll be quite a catch when my top lip has healed. And this brace isn't for ever. Box no. 7432.

 If we share a bath together I have to insist on wearing verruca socks. Woman, 36, still reeling from a school swimming incident in 1975 (six months of padded plasters isn't easy to get over). Box no. 3186.

 I'll see you at the *LRB* singles night. I'll be the one breathing heavily and stroking my thighs by the 'art' books. Asthmatic, varicosed F (93) seeks M to 30 with enough puff in him to push me uphill to the post office. This is not a euphemism. Box no. 4632.

Mature gentleman (62), aged well, noble grey looks, fit and active, sound mind and unfazed by the fickle demands of modern society seeks… damn it, I have to pee again. Box no. 4143.

 These ads try too hard to be funny. Not me, I'm a natural. Juggling, monkey-faced idiot (M, 36). Box no. 5312.

 Toilet duties. That's where you come in – buxom, 22-year-old, blonde stereotype not shy of adjusting the surgical stockings of 73-year-old misanthrope with poor bladder control. Failing that, just send care-home brochures to box no. 0278.

 Join me for sit-ups in Dairy-Free week! M, 42, big-boned. Box no. 6421.

 Hoxton salad-dodger (42 – my age and my waist; M – my sex not my coat size, that's strictly XL) WLTM LRB chubster with an interest in red meat and mustardy dressings. Free first Tuesday of every month, Slimmer's World every Wednesday. Box no. 1275.

 My animal passions would satisfy any woman, if only it weren't for the filibustering of this damned colon. And the chafing of these infernal hospital sheets. Write now to M, 83, for ward visiting hours and a list of approved solids. Box no. 2377.

 I am the literary event of 2007, or at the very least the most entertaining drunk on my ward. Please visit

(Mon–Thurs, 5–7 p.m., bring chocolate, and gin). F, 41. Box no. 4365.

 I wonder if Clive James⁵ reads these. And if he does, would he find me attractive enough to write to? Hope not, I'm after an early-twenties stud-muffin capable of obscene bedroom gymnastics. Woman, 74, living in perpetual hope (and a care home in Pendle), WLTM nearest thing in an Easy-Up-Chair-equipped bungalow. Box no. 4321.

 Every Christmas, without fail, the *LRB* produces the biggest turkey. This year it's me – monocled, plaid-festooned gadabout, out of place in any relationship, or century, that fails to recognise the comfort of a secure knickerbocker. Please help me. Man, possibly your embarrassing uncle, 51. Box no. 0563.

 If dreams were eagles, I would fly, but they ain't, and that's the reason why. Spend New Year singing into your hairbrush with the Goombay Dance Band and me, bitter publishing marketing exec. (F, 33), too drunk at the office party to keep all my slobber behind my teeth. Golden star that leads to paradise. Like a river's running to the ocean I'll come back to you four thousand miles.⁶ Box no. 6308.

---

5 Writer, poet, essayist and critic. Born 1939.

6 From 'Seven Tears', single released by the Goombay Dance Band, which reached number one in the UK in March 1982.

Most vegetarians complain about missing the taste of bacon. Not me, I complain about my liver disease. And rural postal services. Man, 40. Box no. 3143.

 Either I'm desperately unattractive, or you are all lesbians. Bald, pasty man (61) with nervous tick and unclassifiable skin complaint believes it to be the latter but holds out hope for dominant (yet straight) fems at box no. 1075.

 You'll regret replying to this ad – its owner smells of peas. But if you too live in a care home where the quality of the shower water is poor and access to the bath hoist is determined by an inadequate monthly rotation schedule, then write to flaky 72-year-old man with no recollection of where any of these stains have come from, box no. 4220.

"I've divorced better men than you"

Get out of my space. And quit touching. Otherwise friendly F, 42 (publicity director), wants to get to know you. Box no. 4213 (please include full CV, medical records, five recent bank statements, photo and proof of signature).

Tired of feeling patronised by the ads in this column? Then I'm not the woman for you, little man. Today you may be benighted and insignificant, tomorrow you will be more so. Now off you go. Box no. 2912.

Blah, blah, whatever. Indifferent woman. Go ahead and write. Box no. 3253. Like I care.

Disreputable, mean, ruthless, perverse, hateful wretch. But what do divorce lawyers know? Woman, forties, marketing director for major international publishing firm, London/SE, you'll soon find that I'm the finest fellow breathing. Just take time out to get to know me. Box no. 5313.

Don't send me any poems. Woman, 34. Fed up of getting poems. Box no. 4253.

Beneath this hostile museum curator's exterior lies a hostile museum curator's interior. We meet at the coat check and never – and I mean never – deviate from the mapped route. Zone one: Ancient Egypt. Zone two: The Treasures of Greece. Zone three: guided tours only, keep your hands where I can see them. F, 38. Box no. 3452.

You should know that by placing this advert I've lowered my expectations considerably.
Now even you're in with a chance. Don't blow it by mentioning your mother and your predilection for bluestocking NAAFI-types.[1] Woman, 46, accustomed to disappointment, but not that much. Box no. 2541.

 Your age is immaterial, your looks irrelevant. Your bank balance, on the other hand – let's not joke about with that. Grabbing F (28). Box no. 3652.

 I know you like me – you're just too self-conscious to do anything about it. I blame your overbearing mother. And your lazy eye. It *was* me you were flirting with, wasn't it? Loving, considerate F (34). Box no. 5324.

  From now on I'm only going to reply to my own ads.
That's because I'm funnier and better-looking than any of you. Publicist F, 29. Box no. 5132.

 I've divorced better men than you. And worn more expensive shoes than these. So don't think placing this ad is the biggest come-down I've ever had to make. Sensitive F, 34. Box no. 6322.

 5 September is the anniversary of my divorce. So too are 17 November, 12 January, 8 March and 21 June.

1   NAAFI: Navy, Army and Air Force Institutes, created in 1921 by the British Government to run recreational establishments for Armed Forces personnel and to sell goods and services to servicemen and their families.

Summer is usually much quieter – take advantage of the sunshine and lawyers' vacation periods by dating impatient, money-grabbing PR senior (F, 39). Box no. 2582.

 I butchered three volumes of Seamus Heaney² to produce this ad. Publicity exec. (F, 31). Box no. 2561.

 Meet the new me. Like the old me only less nice after three ads without any sexual intercourse. 42-year-old fruitcake (F). Box no. 2611.

 If you really wanted to get to know me, you'd fly me to Riobamba.³ Tickets and flight itinerary, please, to advantage-taking woman, 41, Staffs. Box no. 2612.

 I'm a Pisces – which makes you and me a bad match, but how about your good-looking friend? Non-committal, easily-distracted, fly-by-night F (35). Sorry, I think I just heard my phone ring. Box no. 2541.

 Jarns, nittles, grawlix and quimp!⁴ This column gets more profane with every issue. Strait-laced, bluestocking F seeks to establish higher standard with well-heeled gentleman to 60 with some degree of euphemistic dexterity when the moment demands it,

---

2 Irish poet and lecturer, born 13 April 1939. Heaney has published fifteen volumes of verse, five volumes of translation, six volumes of essays and two plays.

3 A city in Ecuador, 200km south of the capital, Quito. It has a population of 130,000 and an economy based primarily on agriculture.

4 Squiggles used to represent curses in comic books.

and a liberal application of silence when it doesn't. We sleep in separate rooms and never share a towel at box no. 5321.

 Arty, well-read, gorgeous, blonde woman (29), currently working in publishing, WLTM intelligent, sensitive man to 35. Thumb this ad with nervous excitement any more than you already are and you'll end up with a yeast infection. Box no. 6212.

 Male readers of the *LRB*: trawling for sex as your opening gambit doesn't really work. Talk to me about your favourite author; the painting that means the most to you; what smells remind you of your childhood; the day you first saw your parents differently; your first holiday; your favourite place to read; the last recipe you followed; the most recent newspaper clipping you kept; the name of a lover you most recently remembered; your favourite stretch of water; what you like most about Paris or Rome or London; the last time you fed ducks on a pond. Actually, I'm short on time, go ahead and trawl. Woman, 39. Publishing. Get on with it. Box no. 5201.

 Every time I read these ads I cringe with the knowledge that they are all me. And some are you. And we'll probably end up liking each other very much. But let me tell you now, you're not the sort of man I'd normally get off with (he's reading the *Condé Nast Traveller*). You'll do for now, though, but no tongues, and careful where you put those hands. Box no. 7231.

'No,' I said, 'this is comedy,' and threw the biscotti – and his skinny mocha latte – right back in his face. Edgy, humourless F, 41, banned from most train-station Costas. Strangely alone at box no. 6323.

CONGRATULATIONS! You are the thousandth reader to pass this ad by. Your prize is to pay for dinner and listen to me bitch about my university colleagues until pub turfing-out time.[5] And no, you don't get sex. Ever. Ever, ever, ever. Sensitive F, 38. Box no 7382.

---

5   11.30 p.m. in the UK before the introduction of new licensing laws in November 2005.

"Last time I had
this much fun,
I was on forty
tablets a day**"**

Man, 42, suffers severe mood swings. You've got to laugh. On second thoughts, don't. Box no. 7535.

 Today just isn't my day. Neither was yesterday. Tomorrow will be worse. I'm putting all my money on Thursday week. Also my ex-wife's car and my children's tuition fees for 2005–08. Compulsive gambler (M, 53) seeks either love or sound racing tips. Or both. Though strictly speaking the latter generally results in the former. Do we kiss now or later? Box no. 3698.

 Shy, ugly man, fond of extended periods of self-pity, middle-aged, flatulent and overweight, seeks the impossible. Box no. 8623.

 Mignonette is the most beautiful word in the world and I'll deck anyone who says it isn't. Edgy yet playful poet (M, 38). Box no. 7975.

 Leather trousers? Rides on the backs of motorbikes? Bleached hair? Implausible bikinis? Toy boys? It's the menopause – get a grip. Bald male help (53) at box no. 3201.

 I only enjoy this paper when I'm drunk. Teetotal male, 41. Sober since his first (and last) direct-debit instalment three months ago (I've had tattoos and shotgun marriages I've regretted less). Box no. 8200.

 I write the best literature this country's ever seen. Then my spell-checker tells me to kill, kill, kill. No sudden movements with highly-strung F, 38, Reading. Box no. 3627.

 Don't let distance come between us. Or metal bars. Or restricted access. Or the magic sweeties that make the night terrors go away. Write now to bubbly (others say 'Maximum Security' but what do they know?) F, 34, before the clowns tell her to do things that clowns shouldn't do. Box no. 7635.

 Last time I had this much fun, I was on forty tablets a day. It's all downhill from here, so reply to edgy woman, 36, before the good times come to an abrupt halt and the prescriptions finally dry up. Box no. 2596.

 Literary agents! Save time when considering a manuscript by not bothering to read it all. Instead, set two beetles to race across the front page – one, a crippled, three-legged blind beetle named 'Accept', the other a steroid-taking model of beetle athleticism, wearing the very best beetle roller-skates, being pulled by a team of 16 beetle-sized horses and called 'Destroy Every Dream This Man Ever Had'. Whichever beetle wins decides the fate of the author. For a full set of rules and a licence to play (patent pending), write to sobbing, separated, newly alcoholic, chain-smoking man, 38, on pills for his nerves. Box no. 3524.

 Beer Barrel Polka, Pennsylvania Polka, Rain Rain Polka, Mountaineer Polka, Please Help Me, Three Dollar Polka, Who Stole the Kishka Polka, Oh God Help Me, Johnny's Knocking Polka, Two Step Czardas,

Somebody Please Help, Parobek Czardas, Matka
Waltz, Sailor Boy Polka, In The Name of God Won't
Somebody Help Me, Horse Horosza, Young Years
Polka, Silver Slipper Polka, Please Anybody, Ferry Boat
Polka, My Garden Polka, Please, Clarinet Polka, Hu La
La Polka. Box no. 3698.

 We brushed hands in the British Library, then
again in the London Review Bookshop, reaching for
Musil. And then once more on the tube, getting off at
Ladbroke Grove. Serial random hand-brusher (F, 32,
publicity exec.) demands attention, followed by more
attention, followed by extended periods of self-pity.
It's all me, me, me at box no. 8537.

 Publishers! Save time when considering new book
recommendations by submerging literary agents
completely in water. Those who drown will have been
essentially good souls and should be prayed for, whilst
those who live will be witches and must be burned
at the stake. Lonely man, too poor to buy food, his
own children refuse to talk to him, 38, on pills for his
nerves. Box no. 6322.

 Medication-free after all these years! Join me
(anxious, overweight, self-harming flautist, F, 34) for
congratulatory drink (or seven) in side-ward of the
nation's finest. Box no. 4425.

 **So many men to choose from, so few vitamin
supplements.** Arthritic F, 73. Box no. 6133.

There's enough lithium in my medicine cabinet to power three electric cars across a sizeable desert.[1] I'm more than aware that this isn't actually a selling point, but none the less it's my favourite statistic about me. Man, 33 – officially Three Cars Crazy. Box no. 2609.

 I always begin the *LRB* at the personals. Then I drink. Then I weep. Then I move on to the articles. I drink some more. I weep some more. Then I hit the letters page. You can see where I'm heading here? That's right, it's straight to the claims court and if these personal ads don't get any better I'm going to sue each and every one of you. Depressed, anxious, alcoholic M (41) means business, so too does his legal representation (M, 38, cha-cha enthusiast, and M, 42, bit of a chubster but cute to boot). Box no. 6334.

 'Look, Mother, I'm sorry for failing my medical exams, but not being a doctor doesn't make me any less of a son.' Tired of partners who talk in their sleep? Meet insomniac woman (51), who's heard it all before. If you sleep like a log, or currently take lots of medication after 10 p.m., write to me and we can both get some rest. Box no. 4312.

---

1 Lithium-based compounds such as lithium carbonate (Li_2CO_3) are used in medicines to treat some manic-depressive disorders. Lithium is also sometimes used as battery anode material (high electrochemical potential) and lithium compounds are used in dry cells and storage batteries.

Too much sex, not enough vitamin B12.[2] Vegan love-god on the brink of mental and physical collapse (M, 26) seeks pallid, calcium-deficient F for nights of apathy, depression and headaches whilst touring the moral high ground. It's all faux-fur, acrylics and rehydrated soya at box no. 7633.

 Take the last train to Clarksville and I'll meet you at the station.[3] Unless the 10.15 to Watney[4] has been delayed. In which case I'll get the bus – meet me at Morrisons, by the front entrance. If you can't find your way there, get a taxi and I'll give you the fare when I arrive, but make sure you take some change with you. If you don't have any change, take a trumpet so that you can busk for some. Woman, 38, burdened by the need to make contingency plans, seeks well-ordered man to 45. Or woman to 50. Or anyone to 60. Write to box no. 3485. If you can't find stamps, place an ad here and I'll get back to you. If the office is closed, email it. If you can't write, send a taped voice message. Etc., etc.

 Woman, 56, much happier now. Currently at peace with herself and the world. Seeks dependable significant other who doesn't mind listening. Must like cats and darkness. Box no. 7322.

2   A member of the vitamin B complex. It contains cobalt, and so is also known as cobalamin. Vitamin B12 is necessary for the synthesis of red blood cells, the maintenance of the nervous system, and growth and development in children. Deficiency can cause anaemia.

3   'Last Train to Clarksville': the first single recorded by the Monkees. Released 1966.

4   Market in London's East End. Served by three underground stations: Shadwell, Wapping and Whitechapel.

Menopause made me subscribe to this magazine, and I haven't looked back since (although I also came out this morning with no knickers and my bra on outside my jersey). Hormones-a-go-go with flushed woman (54), putting the tins in the fridge at box no. 2534.

 Lessee, whaddwegodheeer??? Looks pretty, smells pretty, and takes me to the places I've only ever dreamt of going. Self-prescribing physician of lurve. Come on in, the shrooms[5] are lovely. Man (that's Dr Man, lady) 98. Box no. 6319.

 I buy all my goods from catalogues specialising in mock Victoriana and post-war trinkets. And I fully expect you to join me in table billiards, charades and Sunday Bible-reading. Strait-laced, edgy F (42) keeping rationing alive in a jolly nostalgia sense while specialists deliberate the correct course of treatment. Box no. 5312.

 Five things I can't live without: the smell of lavender in my garden; eagerly awaited summers; the films of David Lean; my subscription to the LRB; my alone time between the hours of 4.30 p.m. and midnight – if you speak during that time I must kill you. Edgy publicist (F, 35) requires a large berth and mucho sedation three out of every four weeks. Box no. 5298.

---

5   Psilocybin/psilocin-containing mushroom that produces similar effects to LSD when ingested. Also known as 'magic mushrooms'.

Heaven must be missing an angel. If you find her, tell her she bumped my car whilst trying to park her moronic, disco-blaring VW Beetle idiot mobile outside my flat during the early hours of Sunday morning. Insurance details, please, to touchy archivist desperate for a good night's sleep in N1. Box no. 5897.

 The placing of this advert has less to do with me wanting to find love and more to do with me being an attention whore. Reply now before I'm forced to cartwheel at the next London Review Bookshop reading. Woman, 34. Box no. 7664.

 Checking the winning Premium Bonds on Ceefax (page 290)[6] – that's as active as my monthly cycle gets. Post-HRT *Woman's Weekly* defector and overcautious wannabe gambler seeks herbalist with some knowledge of racing form. Finally the years of wild living have arrived. Box no. 4487.

 Stop that damn whistling! The decorators are always in with hypertensive publishing F (34), on the look-out for evening primrose oil[7] smuggler. Box no. 2801.

---

6 Teletext information service provided by the BBC. The name stems from a phonetical representation of 'see facts'.

7 Nutritional supplement and a member of the essential fatty acid (EFA) group. Rich in Omega-6 fatty acids including gamma linolenic acid (GLA), which has certain medicinal properties that may act as an anti-inflammatory for conditions such as arthritis, eczema, high blood pressure and hypertension. Evening primrose oil is also believed to help alleviate cramps associated with pre-menstrual symptoms, though this has yet to be scientifically proven.

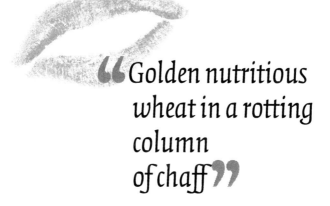

"Golden nutritious wheat in a rotting column of chaff"

I have created an Excel spreadsheet to document all the lovers I've had in my lifetime; the duration of each relationship; and how much each affair cost me in financial terms. I'd like you to be cell A2; forty years; nothing – we'll have independent incomes. IT consultant (M), 34. Box no. 7322.

 The far-too-clever-by-half personal ad. I won't pretend to think you understand. And neither should you (easily impressed woman to forty who knows when not to question a man's Latin and knowledge of sea-bass mating seasons).[1] Box no. 2753.

 Unashamed triumphalist male for the past 46 years. Will I bore you? Probably. Do I care? Probably not. Box no. 4002.

 I once found the perfect match in this column, but it turned out to be an ad I'd written two years earlier that they'd forgotten to publish. Still, you have to admire my consistency. Man, 43. Consistent. Admiring. Admirable. Box no. 4321.

 Christmas all alone? Unwrapping presents you gave yourself? Bernard Matthews oven-ready? Your troubles are over in the shape of obnoxious, drunkard uncle for hire (62). Belches the national anthem in three octaves, scratches inappropriately and is seemingly never satisfied by your very best efforts. Is dinner ready

---

1 Spring (UK, offshore).

yet – and if not, why not? December will be magic
again at box no. 5610.

 Bastard. Complete and utter. Whatever you do, don't
reply – you'll only regret it. (Man, 38.) Box no. 2817.

 **Without love, it doesn't matter if you have all the
qualifications in the world.** Which I have. Please
write for full list. I also have all the money in the world
and look like Jude Law. Yes, I can provide a photo. M,
71, Ottershaw. When named I am the man apart. Box
no. 4319.

 Narcissistic man, 32. If you're better-looking than me
(and I doubt it), why not write? Box no. 6511.

 True love travels on a gravel road. Not in
Cardiganshire – it travels on dirt tracks up unfeasibly
steep hills littered with sheep shit. There's my house,
right at the top. Come on in, the fire's warm and
the roof's just been replaced (it carries a five-year
guarantee against leaks). Simple man, 58, of simple
means. Don't expect a welcoming party. Box no. 3290.

 Google-search this: 'Inherited wealth real estate
Bentley' – that's me, result 63 of 275. It'll take 0.21
seconds to find me online, but an eternity of heartache
in real life. Save time now by writing to box no. 4511,
or by just giving up. Mother says you'll never be good
enough for me anyway. And you carry the odour of
your class.

In June 2001, Laura Buxton released a balloon during
her grandparents' golden-wedding anniversary
celebrations in Staffordshire. She'd attached to it her
name and address along with a note asking the finder
to write back. Ten days later she received a reply. The
balloon had been found by another Laura Buxton in
Wiltshire, 140 miles away. Both Lauras were aged 10
and both had a three-year-old black Labrador, a guinea
pig and a rabbit. The replies to my personal ads are
of a very similar nature, always coming from people
who share my name and major characteristics of my
life. The only distinction is that my replies do actually
come from me. It's not because I have a poor memory
and respond to adverts I don't remember placing, but
because I'm so damned attractive I find me irresistible.
You will too, but if you don't own a three-year-old
black Labrador, a guinea pig and a rabbit I won't reply.
Man. Gorgeous man. 37. Lovely. Kettering. Adorable.
Yummy. Reply soon. Of course I will, you silly little
pussycat. Box no. 2541.

 Ah – to return to student days! Private Tuscan villas,
carefree womanising, yachting and riding the horses
on Father's orchard. Moneyed M (51) will make you
aware of it at every opportunity, and then blame you
for his downfall and current penury. Are you proud of
dragging me down to your level? Maybe not now, but
give it a month or so after you've replied to box no.
4736.

 This ad is not an attempt to find a partner. It is a
Guinness attempt at a record number of rejections.

Realistically, however, I'll probably fail, being as I'm the most gorgeous man in here, have better hair than everybody else, and am fluent in seventeen languages (of which half are no longer in use). Man, 32. Golden nutritious wheat in a rotting column of chaff. Box no. 7552.

 You're not the hottest property on the party circuit. You're a simple-minded publicity bint like all the other girls in the room. But, damn it, don't your eyes just sparkle beneath those tinted one-day Acuvues? Man, 28. Box no. 4789.

 I like my women the way I like my kebab. Found by surprise after a drunken night out and covered in too much tahini. Before long I'll have discarded you on the pavement of life, but until then you're the perfect complement to a perfect evening. Man, 32. Rarely produces winning metaphors. Box no. 5632.

 Damn it. Do all relationships have to end with a trip to the emergency room and a tube of Savlon? Romantic man, 36, seeks pretty little lady to cook the dinner, bring him beer, and surrender her right to orgasm. Box no. 3741.

 Man (53) in 16th year of having relationships with women whose name forms part of a song title WLTM anyone called Eloise, Renee, Delilah, Clementine or

Black Betty.² Age unimportant, but a photo, a birth
certificate and a place on the electoral roll most
certainly are. Box no. 8631.

 Slip your hand into two top corners of the sheet.
With one hand inside each of the top two corners,
fold the sheet (right sides together). Slip each of the
top corners into one of the bottom corners. Lay sheet
on bed or table. Arrange and fold the corners neatly.
Turn in selvages enough to make four straight sides.
Fold in half, then in half again. (All four corners will
be stacked together, and sheet will be in a long strip.)
Then fold the long strip in half, then in half (or thirds,
depending on the size of the sheet) again to make
a square. Sheet should be a compact, neat square.
Smooth and place on shelf. After that, dinner; then I
may consider foreplay. You can call me Brigadier. M,
62. Likes things just so. Box no. 7441.

 In a certain light I look like Robert Mitchum. In a
certain light you look like Kim Novak. More usually I
look like Shrek. More usually you still look like Kim
Novak. Yes, you're very unlucky. Now pass me the
Doritos³ and get over it. Box no. 3917.

2 'Eloise': released by Barry Ryan, 1968; 'Walk Away Renee':
originally recorded by the Left Banke in 1966, then a hit for the Four
Tops in 1968; 'Delilah': a hit for Tom Jones in 1968; 'Clementine':
the advertiser is thought to be referring here to Tom Lehrer's version
appearing on the album *An Evening Wasted With Tom Lehrer*, 1959;
'Black Betty': African-American work song often credited to Huddie
"Leadbelly" Ledbetter, notable recordings include those by Nick Cave
and the Bad Seeds (1986) and Tom Jones (2002).

3 Corn-based crisp snack.

Perennial Teletext-letter writer (M, 43, Lancs).
There's more sex in that statement than you could
possibly imagine. Page 346 tonight, tomorrow night,
and every night for the rest of your life (the red button
if you have Fastext). Box no. 9461.

 I'm the one that you want. Unfortunately, though, I
fancy your mate. Could you give her my number? Box
no. 9573. Cheers.

 Tell me your dreams. I'll laugh at them all, you silly
little pussycat, and quickly prove how unlikely you
are to achieve them. You won't need to – I'm the most
successful and handsome man you'll ever be lucky
enough to meet. Now be a dear and put the kettle on.
Box no. 8362.

 Commit your fondest memories to tape. Then
discard them all, you harlot – I should be all you
need. You come baggage-free or you don't come at
all. Obsessive, jealous, paranoid nut-case (M, 58).
Otherwise quite decent and happy at box no. 9375.

 When you do that voodoo that you do so well, I
invoke 16th-century witchcraft laws and have you
burned at the stake. No shenanigans with Quaker M,
39, at box no. 2741.

 **Whatever you're looking for, you won't find it in
any of these other ads.** But if you like early-morning
trips down the Thames, Sunday-morning pastries,
Saturday afternoons in Richmond Park and spur-

of-the-moment trips to Scotland, then join me,
sensitive M, 48. I won't be participating in any of these
sojourns, because most of my time is spent journaling
the activities of my neighbours for the daily reports I
submit to my local council as part of my ongoing war
against sound pollution and overhanging conifers. But
you should be made aware of the options open to you
if my vigilance becomes inexplicably tiresome to you.
By that point, of course, it will be too late and you'll
have become one of Them. It's only a matter of time
before you have your own paragraphs in my report.
The pencil is always sharpened at box no. 9390.

 You are going to be alone this Christmas. That's
because nobody likes you. I, however, will provide you
with a basic meal and some pleasant company on the
understanding that you do not criticise my collection
of antique medical implements. Tidy man, 51. Size 9
slipper.[4] Box no. 7314.

 I laugh at my own jokes. They're all about you. Many
levels of arseholery with publishing M, 43. Box no.
8946.

  Romance is dead. So is my mother. Man, 42,
inherited wealth. Box no. 7652.

 List your ten favourite albums. I don't want to
compare notes, I just want to know if there's anything

---

4   9.5 US equivalent.

worth keeping when we finally break up. Practical, forward-thinking man, 35. Box no. 8089.

 People who use museum postcards instead of letter paper; people who own garden composters; ticket collectors who cannot accept the idea of the bloke in the kiosk at the station disappearing to the toilet at the exact time you've arrived to buy your fare; mechanics called Andy who get stroppy over the phone if you call during their lunch hour, fully expecting you to know that they take lunch between 10 and 11 in the morning; Islington intellectuals who have named their children 'Billy' or 'Eddy' despite knowing full well that they will never spend any time in William Hill's waiting to hear what the going is like at Haydock; people from Bellway estates in Swindon who have named their children 'Mariella' or 'Giles' despite knowing full well that they are going to spend most of their adult lives in William Hill's waiting to hear what the going is like at Haydock; people who shoehorn obscure French novelists into any conversation; people who take oversized stroller pushchairs on the Northern Line at rush hour and get shirty when other passengers refuse to dislocate their limbs and fold themselves up in the corner to make room; newspaper supplement journalists who begin every article like they're writing a novel in the hope that a literary agent will snap them up; literary agents who snap up newspaper-supplement journalists believing that their opening paragraphs would make an excellent start to a novel; the girl at Superdrug who never tells me how much my items come to but expects me to succumb to the power

of her mind and makes me look at the little screen
on her till instead; postmen who make a concerted
effort to bend packages with 'DO NOT BEND' clearly
stamped across the front; people who go to public
schools named after German saints and attend *Rocky*
Horror Picture Show-themed leavers' parties at the end
of their final term, then bore everyone they know
for years to come about what a 'seriously good larf'
it was; thirty-somethings who listen to Radiohead,
believing that Thom Yorke's depressing introspection
has revolutionised the British music scene and made
rock energetic once again without realising that Dire
Straits fans were saying exactly the same thing about
them in the early eighties; people who buy organic
mushrooms; people who subscribe to magazines and
get excited every time a new one lands on the doormat;
people who have doormats; people who applaud
the linesman's offside flag; people with espresso
machines bought from Index for £19.99 who make
you drink the stuff whenever you go round, then go on
about the difference in quality and how you can 'really
taste the bean' although it's no different from Mellow
Birds but takes four times as long to produce; people
with more than one cat; people who have bought
radiator covers; people who frame museum postcards
sent by people who use them instead of letter paper;
people who own a copy of Michael Palin's *Pole to Pole*
on DVD. Everybody else write to man, 37. Box no.
6879.

" I once came within an ace of making my own toothpaste **"**

Thorium is a radioactive metallic element used in X-ray tubes, photoelectric cells and sunlamps. Its isotope thorium-232 is used as a nuclear fuel in breeder reactors. The guy no one wants to be faced with in Scrabble (48) seeks hopeless Kerplunk and Buckaroo contestant to make my superiority at board games complete (I happily concede at Twister, although, strictly speaking, that's not a board game).[1] Box no. 8647.

 Huge frontal lobes and hyperactive Broca's area,[2] in cute casing, seeks non-mutant XY genotype (forties, fifties) with intact cortico-limbic connections and own teeth. Box no. 8064.

 Burned by the nuclear reactor of love, bruised by the capacitor of reason, chafed by the nylon seam of romance. Passion's own engineer (that's you,

[1] Kerplunk: family game in which contestants have to take turns to remove straws from a plastic tube without dropping any of the marbles suspended above. First released by the Ideal toy company in 1967. Buckaroo: game consisting of a spring-loaded plastic mule. Contestants take turns to load the mule with various gold-mining items. The loser is the player who triggers the spring action, causing the mule to kick off any items loaded on to its plastic saddle. First released by Milton Bradley Games in 1970. Twister: described as 'sex in a box' on its first release by M.B. Games in 1966, Twister became hugely popular after being featured on US television's *The Tonight Show*, on which Eva Gabor joined Johnny Carson in a game. Contestants play on a large plastic sheet covered with big coloured circles. A board with a spinning wheel is used to determine where players must place each hand and foot, often with players collapsing on one another. Requires two or more players. None of these games uses batteries.

[2] Area of the brain involved with language-processing, speech production and comprehension.

emotionally strong F to 50, own 4x4 and love of
Timberland stores) needed by the mechanic of shame
(that's me – timid M, 45, Ethel Austin undergarments
and moccasins slightly worn under the left sole owing
to a camber developed in my calliper-wearing years at
St Bede's Elementary). Box no. 8543.

 Gynotikolobomassophile (M, 43) seeks
neanimorphic F to 60 to share euneirophrenia. Must
enjoy pissing off librarians (and be able to provide the
correct term for same). Box no. 4732.

 In all organisms, the precise control of the expression
of the many thousands of genes comprising their
genomes is essential for correct development, growth
and function. That's the rule, now meet the exception.
Man, 43. Sharks in the gene pool, cell dysregulation
and DNA-a-go-go with button-down, beardy
biochemist. Divide and proliferate inappropriately at
box no. 5809.

 **I pull all the right levers and push all the right
buttons**, all in the correct order, and still my computer
produces this loser of an advert. Fortunately my
Tyneside jambalaya will save me (M, 43), and you (M
to 50), from having to worry about anything more
technological than bits of crabstick between my teeth.
Pick guitar, fill fruit jar and be gay-o[3] at box no. 4566.

---

3 Taken from the song 'Jambalaya' by country singer/songwriter
Hank Williams. In 1952 Jo 'GI Jo' Stafford's cover reached number
eleven in the UK charts.

Boanthropist (M, 34) seeks bovine woman with udders and bell. Box no. 7986.

 Seismic geometry is number forty-three in my list of vices. Name one other and I'll marry you. Pleading, needy, yet resolutely square M (38) WLTM any female who isn't my mother. Box no. 7553.

 M, 34, WLTM F to 30 able scientifically to prove the validity of the ten-second rule concerning dropped food. Box no. 9713.

 Computer scientist currently researching denotational semantics, maps programming and relationships between linear lambda-calculi and their models. I bait you, I lure you, then I reel you in like the fish you are. M (that's Dr M, girlfriend), 36. Box no. 6843.

 Just how useful are radioisotopes in determining your ideal partner? Reply to amphetamine-fuelled love professor (M, 81) immediately to take the test of your lifetime. Box no. 5390.

 Know your thermocouple accuracy table, then love me like the fool you are. Geo-sex daddy of the rhodium-refining world (M, 62) seeks practically anyone. Anyone at all. I mean it. Please. Anyone. Box no. 7809.

 Nothing in this world makes sense. Apart from *Sphenodon punctatus*, last survivor of the reptilian order

Rhynchocephalia. If only there were a woman like it
– cold, efficient and brutal in love, but also able to feed
off small animals, inhabit the breeding burrows of
certain small petrels and be in possession of a vestigial
third eye. Zoologist, M (51), possibly a little too close
to his work. And his mother. Box no. 8643.

 Male otolaryngologist (39) seeks woman with
normal-shaped head. Box no. 7598.

 Come on everybody! C-C-C-Come on everybody!
Lecturer in Linguistics and Philosophy (M, 38) seeks
F to 35 with interests in the subfield of morphosyntax
and theories of distributed morphology. Replies,
and details of major published works, please, to Jive
Bunny, J-J-J-Jive Bunny,[4] box no. 4332.

 **Researchers at the Australian National
University** recently employed a technique called
electromagnetically induced transparency, in which
a beam of laser light puts the atoms in a solid sample
into a state in which a signal light pulse can be
trapped. They succeeded in stopping light for more
than one second. Despite this remarkable advance
in science and technology, I still can't get a man. If
you can explain why in 2,000 words or less, I'll share
my ideas for nuclear toast extraction with you. And
possibly have sex. Woman, 41. Intelligent, austere

4   Jive Bunny and the Mastermixers. Pop act that used sampling
techniques and synthesisers combining with classic swing tracks. Had
three consecutive number ones in the UK between July and December
1989.

and mentally-troubled like all good forty-something women should be. Box no. 7532.

 Only the good die young. And sea-monkeys. Providing you flush them. Reclaim those years of bitter disappointment, waiting for the turgid little insects of your life to blossom into entertaining webbed-toed critters, with good, honest cephalopod (35). Underwater kingdom and X-ray specs available from box no. 5789.

 Not allowed to compete in the 2004 RoboCup Robot Soccer World Cup[5] with his team of bionically improved cats, computer geek and amateur biomechanic (M, 32) seeks woman to 30 with knowledge of advanced humanoid circuit systems to assist in the building of electronic water-loving mammal capable of writing children's fantasy fiction (or The RobOtter Potter-Jotter®, to use the project's full name). Must also have large bust. No loons. Box no. 8677.

 They all laughed at Christopher Columbus. Freelance astronomer (male, 47) can prove the universe is shaped like a big egg. All he needs is the love of a good woman, and £40,000. Cheques and billets-doux to box no. 3719.

---

5 International project to promote artificial intelligence. The first official games were held in Nagoya, Japan, in July 1997.

Behold the Polymath of Love. Don't get too near, though, because you'll trigger my nervous asthma. Man (34). Box no. 5478.

 I once came within an ace of making my own toothpaste. Man, 36, seeks woman with knowledge of fluoride compounds/tantric love-making. Box no. 5987.

"Vodka, canasta,
evenings in,
and cold, cold
revenge"

My favourite Ben & Jerry's is Acid-Boiled Bones of Divorce Lawyer. They don't yet make it, but, damn, I can taste its sweet, sweet ice-creamy softness already. Bed-sit-living doctor (M, 54). Box no. 6321.

 Your stars for today: a pretty Cancerian (35) will cook you a lovely meal, caress your hair softly, then squeeze every damn penny from your adulterous bank account before slashing the tyres of your Beamer. Let that serve as a warning. Now then, risotto? Box no. 7394.

 In the next Saul Bellow[1] book, the hero dies in the end. Spoiler of plots (ex-fiction-reviewer, working my way up to children's TV, M, 62) WLTM woman impressed by collections of badly-received proof editions. Who knows what tomorrow brings? I do – this tale ends with your falling hopelessly in love with me until I have another affair and you stab me mercilessly through the heart with the plastic spork[2] you kept from our first meeting (it was at a Spudulike[3] in Gloucester; you had chicken supreme and I had the chilli-non-carne vegetarian option). Box no. 6213.

 Save it – anything you've got to say can be said to my lawyer. But if you're not my ex-wife, why not write to box no. 5377. I enjoy vodka, canasta, evenings in, and cold, cold revenge.

---

1 Author and winner of the 1976 Nobel Prize for Literature. Died 5 April 2005, some years after this ad was submitted.

2 Plastic eating implement comprising a fork and a spoon in a single device.

3 Fast-food outlet specialising in potatoes.

The last thing I want to do when ending our relationship is meet up at Waterstone's Piccadilly to muse about the fun we had – mine's a skinny mocha latte – but now it's time to move on – and can I have a Danish with that, please? Either we end it in a coffee bar in Milan – and you get the bill (including flights and transfers) – or we don't end it at all. F, expects no emotional commitment from you, so don't think I'm bothered by your lack of attention and over-devotion to your work/friends/TV. Break my heart, then leave me – you're no different from the others. Fun, fun, fun at box no. 8321.

 'I was in the war, you know.' This and other tales of mind-numbing emptiness from incontinent father (81) of 'ungrateful turd' of a son (46) stupid enough not to change the locks on his Barnstead semi back in 1991 when his wife and kids were still with him and nursing-home saving schemes had yet to go tits-up. Kick me at box no. 4190.

 Synopsis: thirty-something man places lonely heart in literary magazine. He gets a couple of replies, none of them really worth considering, until one day a scented letter arrives. He opens it, not really expecting much, but is surprised to find a few brief paragraphs that genuinely touch him. Could this be the one? She sounds perfect – is roughly the same age as him, well educated, attractive, cultured (likes theatre, travel, poetry-reading), and is as enthusiastic about cookery as he is. They decide to meet up and sure enough they have a great time; he invites her back to his Oxford apartment, and after a few liaisons, some crazy love-making and waking up a few Sundays together to stare at the oak trees through the bedroom window they decide to move in together. Here's the twist: only at this juncture – when his Santana and King Crimson[4] albums have mysteriously turned up at the local Oxfam shop and his Japanese film poster collection has been replaced with pictures of sad clowns – does he discover that at some point in her life she's had her brain removed by aliens and had it replaced with rabid ants. Sound familiar? Then join me, 34-year-old man with recent spinal injuries from having to spend the last six weeks on his own two-seater sofa in his own apartment while crazy lady enjoys the sort of sleep that only lithium[5] can invoke in his own king-size bed. Box no. 7278. References essential. Also full medication history.

 If my Christmas present this year is a gift subscription to *History Today* I'm going to be pissed off. Then I'm going to get pissed. Then I'm going to divorce you. You know who you are. Perfume, lingerie, nice womanly things, please, to your wife at box no. 6824.

 They should get a divorce lawyer to sponsor this column. After all, it's paid for by the blood, sweat and tears of the beaten, dejected, lost and all-too-often twice-married. Twice-married man (51, Shropshire).

---

4 Progressive rock band, formed 1969.

5 See p. 36, n. 1.

Beaten, dejected, lost. Hoping to win use of a divorce lawyer. Box no. 8717.

 Did you know that 82% of male *LRB* readers are deadly ninja assassins? I'm not one of them, however, because my kung fu is of an older school, whose secrets are known only to a select few. Not only can I summon chi demons with a whisper, but also I live in my parents' spare room and harbour impotent revenge fantasies against my ex-wife's lawyer. This latter move is known in ancient kung fu circles as 'mardy locust'. Let me teach you its deadly glare. Pathetic man, 41. Harrow. Box no. 9768.

  Box no. 0408. I missed my period. Box no. 7546.

 A girlfriend isn't a girlfriend unless she makes my mother cry with grief every time she visits. For two years now she's sat, contented, in front of the TV with not a care in the world. That's where you come in. Professional M, 38, seeks heartless common slut with no small knowledge of sheltered-housing application procedures. Basingstoke. Box no. 7442.

Summer, 1974. Everybody was kung fu fighting.[6] Not me, I was revising the sociology of Paulo Freire. Who's laughing now, sixth-formers of Sherbourne Fields

---

6 'Kung Fu Fighting': single released by Carl Douglas in 1974. Reached number one on both sides of the Atlantic and sold nine million copies.

School, Coundon? Mortgage-free M and perennial
Friends Reunited[7] outcast. Box no. 2776.

 All I need is the air that I breathe and to love you.[8]
And a five-door saloon (fully air-con). And a minimum
income of £55K per annum. And two holidays a year
(Latin America plus one other of my choosing). If you
can meet these requirements, apply to 'Evil Dragon
Lady, Breaker of Men's Constitutions' (37), box no.
3685.

 Put me anywhere but next to him. Or her. And I
haven't said a word to them since 1987. Divorced
woman, 58. The single most difficult relative to sit at
weddings. Give it your best shot, but for Christ's sake
straighten your tie first, at box no. 7535.

---

7   UK internet-based service whereby users can measure their own
success in life by assessing the comparative failures of their school
colleagues.

8   From 'The Air That I Breathe' (Hammond/Hazlewood). Single
released by the Hollies, January 1974. Reached number two in the
UK charts. The music was utilised by UK pop combo Radiohead on
the 1993 single 'Creep', which lists Hammond and Hazlewood in the
song's credits.

" They call me
naughty Lola "

Defeat is unthinkable. So too are those curtains with that sofa. Interior designer and gay lieutenant in the Army of Love (37). I've faced more battles than you've had hot dinners, Private, and I've never once thought of buying slip-ons. Polish your buttons and dismantle that twisted-willow arrangement at box no. 2486.

 67-year-old disaffiliated flaneur picking my toothless way through the urban sprawl, self-destructive, sliding towards pathos, jacked up on Viagra and on the look-out for a contortionist who plays the trumpet. Box no. 2179.

 Not everyone appearing in this column is a deranged cross-dressing sociopath. Let me know if you find one and I'll strangle him with my bra. Man, 56. Box no. 3221.

 Dress up like a Viking and join me (M, 51) in my York farm-dwelling. Not only will we experience crazy Jorvik mud-love, but we'll get Local Heritage Initiative grant funding. Have cake – eat it. All at box no. 2187.

 Enigmatic-looking woman, 52 – imagine John Sutherland[1] in a bra. It doesn't describe what I look like, but it does give an insight into my evening distractions. Please help. Box no. 3573.

---

1 Columnist, author, lecturer and Emeritus Lord Northcliffe Professor of Modern English Literature of University College, London. In 2005 he was Chair of Judges for the Man Booker Prize.

Mimi, 64, WLTM man whose first name is composed entirely of Roman numeral letters. You must also have a degree in advanced mathematics and be very well endowed. Box no. 2486.

 LRB **personals are the new dogging.** As usual I'm at the back of the car-park with an empty thermos and a broken torch. Make the winter nights shorter and warmer by replying urgently to Thinsulated[2] M, 43, Worcs. Box no. 2579.

 Mid-fifties man. Recently discovered guilt. Can't wait to try it out. Box no. 7297.

 Poet, M, 32. My career demands you break my heart. It also demands you buy all the drinks and have lots of strange sex with me. I'll give you an acknowledgement in my next volume, so it's not an entirely unrewarding relationship. Box no. 1873.

 LRB **personals took my life** and drained it into a bottle of Bell's to be poured down my neck every morning, noon and night. Now I'm back! And kicking up a storm in chiffon and feathers! Join me in my bijou Kingston pied-à-terre for a chorus line of two (I'm the opener – M, 38; you're the encore – private detective to 60 with some experience of wide-angle photography). Box no. 8542.

---

2 Thinsulate: insulated clothing brand.

Slut in the kitchen, chef in the bedroom. Woman
with mixed priorities (37) seeks man who can toss a
good salad. Box no. 7421.

 Shot by both sides[3] – failed bi-curious experiment
(M, 34) seeks Home Counties third alternative
for nights of thinking about sex, but mostly spent
reading. It's always time for cocoa and Jenga in the
awkward silence of box no. 2196.

 The only thing that makes me happy is weeping
in front of the television whilst wearing mother's
clothes. That, and jazzercise.[4] M, 42. There's always
time for guilt, *Newsnight*, and a good abs workout in
the tortured juvenile psyche of box no. 2366.

 ***Aber aus dem Mantel liess das Verhängnis ein
stahlhartes Gehäuse werden.***[5] Wait 'til you see my
nightie. Man, 35. Box no. 5221.

 I am Mr Fantabulous! You are Nurse Twill. Tonight
I will be administering the medicine, and you will be
my very willing patient. Gay dresser (51) seeks fashion
catastrophe to 60 for evenings of making those awful

---

3 'Shot by Both Sides': début single by post-punk band Magazine,
released 1978. Reached number forty-one in the UK charts.

4 Fitness routine based on jazz dance.

5 'Fate decreed that the cloak should become an iron cage.' From *The
Protestant Ethic and the Spirit of Capitalism* by Max Weber.

Susannah and Trinny women choke on their own jealous mauve bile.[6] Box no. 2187.

 Technically, by writing this ad, I'm breaking the terms of my probation. Technically, though, I'm not really a woman either. Two wrongs always make a right in the mixed-up, muddled-up, security-tagged and banned-from-most-Croydon-shopping-centres world of box no. 3692.

 My ideal woman is a man. Sorry, mother. Box no. 6221.

 Click here to sign my guestbook. Amateur nude photographer and Ostend bi-curious swinging M (53) would like to hear your comments as long as they don't include the following: 'photographing from a small height or ladder minimises double chins and shows faces better'; 'keep backgrounds simple and uncluttered'; 'sun over shoulders often provides the best natural light, especially morning and late-afternoon sun'; and 'use good lenses and fresh batteries'. Box no. 3121.

 Baste me in butter and call me Slappy. No, really. M, 35. Box no. 3175.

6   Susannah Constantine and Trinny Woodall. Hosts of the BBC's *What Not to Wear*, a TV series that takes members of the public regardless of shape, height or age and forces them into re-evaluations of their fashion decisions.

It takes a real man to wear a dress. It takes a revolutionary to wear those shoes with that blusher. Box no. 3194.

 Less Venus in Furs, [7] **more Derek in Buxton.** Interested? Write to Derek in Buxton. Box no. 6385.

 I have nothing to offer readers of the *LRB*, other than my expertise in classical literature. Oh, and a Prince Albert.[8] Man, 51. Box no. 6210.

 I have known only shame. Then, last week, I experienced surprise. Man, 37. Box no. 4126.

 They call me Naughty Lola. Run-of-the-mill beardy physicist (M, 46). Box no. 4023.

 I am not afraid to say what I feel. At this moment in time I feel anger, giddiness, and the urge to dress like a bear and forage for berries at motorway hedgerows. Man, 38. Box no. 3632.

---

7 Venus in Furs, 1870 novella by Leopold Ritter von Sacher-Masoch, 1870. Published as part of a larger body of fiction, *The Testament of Cain*. The book details the infatuation of its central character, Severin, with his mistress, Wanda. His desire is to be enslaved and dominated by her, giving rise to the term 'masochism', coined by nineteenth-century psychiatrist Krafft-Ebing.

8 Male genital hoop piercing.

Doorman at the swingers' party of life. Peripheral figure, 43, holding out for more than a left-over goody bag and a handshake. Coruisk.[9] Box no. 4221.

 Always the bridesmaid. Cross-dressing art-history lecturer (M, 37). Surbiton. Box no. 0486.

 I intend to spend the summer stewing over failed relationships. You can join me if you like, but know now that you'll never live up to Sandra, Jackie, Dawn, Helen, Karen or Peter. M, 37. Bitter, bi-curious, Bebington. Box no. 4762.

 When, oh when will they remake *Falcon Crest*?[10] Man, 43. Obviously gay. Duh! Box no. 3721.

 Tonight I'm off to the Baton Rouge to have sexual intercourse with Josephine Baker. Tomorrow I'll be back in Chichester waiting for *Holby City* to start. Archaeologist and perennial *folie du jour* seeks F to 98 for high-kicking, sequined frolics. Box no. 2654.

 This Christmas, I'm hoping for surgical breast enhancement. Man, 45. Join me pre, post, and every pier between. Box no. 7001.

9   Loch set in the middle of the Cuillin Mountains on the Isle of Skye. 'Rarely human eye has known/ A scene so stern as that dread lake,/ With its dark ledge of barren stone.' Sir Walter Scott, *The Lord of the Isles*, 1815.

10   American TV soap opera broadcast between 1981 and 1990 about the feud between two rich Californian wine families, the Channings and the Giobertis.

Yes, sir. I can boogie. Man. Academic. 62. Quite
possibly gay. Box no. 3631.[11]

Gay, wasted Cambridge dandy (M, 48). There are
things in this column that toluene-sniffing afternoons
just can't give. They are all you: Spanish matador, 21,
rural, church-educated mute, body toned by early-
morning farm work in the delicate dew-soaked rays of
Solaris. Box no. 6313.

**Do you have a body like March in the 1997 Pirelli
calendar?** Or like February in Kwik-Fit 1985? Either
way, November from *New Left Review* 1963 would
like to hear from you to discuss pit stops, pressure
absorption, Habermas's vision of Europe and bras.
Box no. 2731.

It only takes a minute, girl. Not to fall in love, but to
realise how futile it is to expect a normal relationship
from these ads. With that in mind I'm after a juggling,
trombone-blowing F in the finest gold lamé this side
of Elvis (you're not a day older than 97). Box no. 1379.

Don't make our love seem light, the future isn't just
one night – it's written in the moonlight and painted
on the stars.[12] Military historian (M, 47). As queer as
teeth. Box no. 6172.

11 'Yes Sir, I Can Boogie': single released by Spanish duet Baccara in
1977. Sold sixteen million copies worldwide, reaching number one in
various countries and resulting in the duet's being listed in the *Guinness
Book of Records* that year as the highest-selling female musical group.

12 Taken from 'Don't Give Up On Us' – single released by David
Soul. Reached number one in the UK charts in 1976.

❝My last chance to get a man fell in autumn, 1992❞

This is the first time in my life I've appeared in any font other than Courier New. That's because my best work is still in my head, as are my years of financial stability, my buff physique, the respect of my peers, and my ability to trim sea bass. What were you expecting – Saul Bellow? Man, 34. Takes what he can get, as will you. Box no. 1763.

 I know, this is neither the time nor the place to mention marriage, but I've always loved you. Whichever one replies first. Man, 56. I've left a space on the mortgage for your name. Are you ready for children yet? Box no. 8221.

 Woman who wanted to marry my dad – you didn't give me any contact details. Don't play games with the desperate. Box no. 1721.

 Speak a foreign language? Evidently I do. Let me try plain English. Me: woman, 38. You: man, not older than forty, not covered in prison tattoos and not currently hospital resident. Savvy? Photos (clothed only) to box no. 5236.

 At Feltham Station turn right on to Hounslow Road. Take the first left on to Hanworth Road, then the third right into Ashfield Avenue. At the second tree on the pavement on the left, next to the red Vauxhall Astra with the out-of-date tax disc, that's where the Spaniards buried the lost treasure of Moctezuma – start digging. You won't find it, but you'll have a better chance at that than of finding love in this column.

Trust me, this is my fifth (and final – all my credit cards have been cancelled) outing. It's always one last throw of the dice for desperate but easily persuaded F, 45, at box no. 6202.

 LRB personals are my only mistress. Night my only friend. I learned that the hard way. But not before I'd paid 80 pence a word for this beauty. Man, 34. Knocking firmly on the door of failure for neither the first nor the last time in his life. Box no. 0378.

 Placing this ad doesn't mean I'm desperate to find a mate. Offering respondents £15 in book tokens, however, does. Man, 37, offering £15 in book tokens to all respondents (must include full résumé, medical history, and proof of being brunette with the same first name as my mother; offer subject to availability and the Child Support Agency not finding out that I have £15 of book tokens in a drawer at home). Box no. 0843.

 My last chance to get a man fell in autumn, 1992. The current window closes four weeks and two days from the publication date of this issue. Hurry up and write. Box no. 1432.

 Allele, anatta, arrear, arrere, bedded, bettee, breere, caccap, ceesse, cobbob, cocoon, deesse, dolool, doodad, effere, emmele, emmene, ennean, essede, feyffe, gaggee, giggit, googol, gregge, hammam, hummum, hubbub, jettee, kokoon, lessee, lesses, mammal, mammee, mossoo, mutuum, nerrer,

ossous, pazazz, pepper, perree, pippin, powwow,
reeder, reefer, reeffe, refeff, retree, seasse, secess,
seesen, sensse, sessle, settee, sissoo, tattee, tattoo,
tedded, teerer, teeter, teethe, terrer, testee, tethee,
tetter, tittee, treete, unnung, veerer, weeded, zaarra.
Six-letter words with one occurrence of one letter, two
occurrences of another letter and three occurrences of
another letter. By Christ, I need a woman. I'm 41, but
if you've got a pulse, cable TV and a smoothie-maker
you'll do. Box no. 4290.

 **Your buying me dinner doesn't mean I'll have sex
with you.** I probably will have sex with you though.
Honesty not an issue with opportunistic male, 38. Box
no. 1898.

 My Christmas Day TV schedule includes a pause in
transmission at 3.52 p.m. for me to cry into the sleeve
of the cardigan I bought myself. Unless you want to
meet up and have crazy post-turkey sex? No? No? Man,
34. Box no. 3287.

 I gambled my reputation, marriage and house on
equine hoof-magnets being the only sure way to
provide electricity once fossil fuels have run out. The
least you could do is gamble on the cost of a second-
class stamp to see if I'm really a 6´ tall Adonis-like
superbrain (which I am, regardless of what my mother
and ex-wife say). Man, 47. Cute as teeth. Derby. Box
no. 0175.

Despite your listing 34 French erotic novels as your favourite reads, I liked you. Then you went and ruined everything by spending an hour ordering continental ales in the voice of Yoda.[1] LRB-reading men, there is surely something for you all to learn from this. I reluctantly accept, however, that most of you will take nothing from today's lesson. Woman, 35, seriously considering going gay unless the standard of replies from this column improves. Box no. 8963.

 Once the excitement of placing this ad has died down, I'll have to face up to the cruel realities of a second mortgage, liver disease and a direct debit that ain't going away. At least I have all those replies to look forward to. Man, 51. Teetering on the edge of the abyss that your cruel silence is going to push him into. Box no. 5732.

 With the money from my article I bought myself a mobile home, so at least I could get some enjoyment out of being alone.[2] They say one swallow doesn't make a summer, meet last winter's ostrich (M, 35, Brentford). Once hopeful bon vivant, now genuine fish out of water, one-time (and I mean one-time) LRB contributor (it was back in 1986 – I'm hanging all my hopes on you remembering it). It didn't get a single

---

1 Jedi Master.

2 Echo of 'Levi Stubbs' Tears', single released by Billy Bragg, 1986. The original lyric is 'With the money from her accident she bought herself a mobile home/ So at least she could get some enjoyment out of being alone'.

mention on the letters page, but you can change that.
Write now to box no. 0442.

 Ploughing the loneliest furrow. Nineteen LRB
personals and counting. Only one reply. It was my
mother telling me not to forget the bread on my way
home from B&Q. Man, 51. Box no. 3708.

 Dancing on the table impresses no one. Except my
mother, but she's in a home and not allowed to watch
the news. Strait-laced guy with low aspirations thinks
you'll do. Box no. 2078.

 Things I won't do for love include replacing
corroding soil pipes and trepanning at home.
Everything else is A-OK. Eager-to-please woman (36)
seeks domineering man to take advantage of her
flagging confidence. Tell me I'm pretty, then watch me
cling, at box no. 3286.

 Celebrate 37 years of me this coming 20 October!
Send cash, candles and intimate items of underwear to
lonely Libran lawyer, Leicester, struggling with some
of life's cruellest alliterations. Box no. 5180.

 ***LRB*-reading women to 40!** Save money on your new
subscription by becoming the lover of 38-year-old
man who has already signed up for next year. I'm only
thinking of you. Box no. 4207.

 East, west, slate is best! Bored roofing-materials
manufacturer looking for a bit of joy in the pages

of the LRB. Obviously I failed. In desperation I turn
to you, single ladies to 50 with more than a passing
interest in gutterings, fascias and polyvinyl sheet
edging. Box no. 1296.

 The pressure exerted on your body if you tried to
read this advert in the hadal regions of the ocean[3]
would be enough to turn you into a hideous slime-
thing with brains dripping out of your ears. Publicity
exec. (F, 28) seeks any type of happiness afforded
by this cold, desolate planet before, without food,
without hope, and with too many Nick Hornby[4] book
endorsements to collect, I fall asleep for ever. Could be
gay for the right woman. Box no. 5212.

 LRB-**reading women to 40!** Save money when
considering soup for dinner by becoming lover of 38-
year-old man who buys plenty of soup but can never
finish the whole tin. I'm only thinking of you. Box no.
1385.

 Will you sleep with me? Knowing is half the
battle. Man, neither the time nor the inclination for
subtleties. Box no. 2574.

 ***Die Rhabarbermarmelade die ich selbst gemacht
habe ist unerreichbar.*** *Was ich brauche ist ein Mann
der gut mit Einmachglasern umgehehen kann. Du solltest*

---

3   Deep sea trenches beginning 6,000 metres below the surface of the
sea and deeper than the abyssal regions (4,000 to 6,000 metres deep).
An extreme environment in which animal life is scarce.

4   Author.

ausserdem selbstgemachten Wein geniessen. Und du wirst mich heiraten sobald du erfährst dass ich schwanger bin mit deinen Zwillingen. Frau, 56.[5] *Box no. 3229.*

Some chances are once in a lifetime. Not this one – I've been in the last 12 issues. Either I strike gold this time or I become a lesbian. Man, 43. Box no. 8504.

Don't speak, you'll only destroy my already low opinion of you. And put your pants back on. And your wig. Terminally disappointed woman (38, Barnstaple) WLTM a man. Form a queue, then I'll negotiate the criteria. Box no. 2106.

Male *LRB* readers. Drawing little faces on your thumbs, getting them to order meals, then shouting at them for not being able to pay is no way to win a woman. You know who you are. Men to 40 with working credit cards, reply to once-bitten, twice-bitten, three-strikes-and-you're-all-out F, 35. Box no. 1379.

If I was a gambling man, I'd bet you'd be blonde, 30, passionate, impetuous and writing poetry. If I trusted my instinct, you'd be brunette, 35, a little cynical, preparing for that year-out sabbatical and writing that first novel. If I left it to fate, you'd be 67, bald and a man with sclerotic arteries. The intuition my mother

---

5 'The quality of my homemade rhubarb marmalade is unsurpassable. What I need is a man who is good with pickling jars. You should also be able to enjoy homemade wines. And you will marry me as soon as you realise I am pregnant with your twins. Woman, 56.'

handed down and my collection of county court judgments suggest that placing an ad in this column puts you firmly in the last category. Resigned M (52, Colchester[6]) finally embracing defeat and anything else that comes along at box no. 4176.

---

6 Town in the east of England. Ordnance Survey grid reference TQ995255. Population 104,390.

"I'm not a vet, but I do enjoy volunteer work"

I'm everything you need times by six and a half.
Divide it by two, now subtract your age, add my
birthday and multiply by the first three digits of your
phone number. That's right – 3´7´´ unemployed
children's Maths-Magic entertainer seeks woman
whose age, height and Barclaycard PIN number are all
multiples of 7. Failing that, you'll do. Box no. 3658.

 My diagnosis? A broken heart. And my prescription?
A poultice of German love. Misunderstood
homeopathic practitioner (M, 38). Anything involving
hands requires my lawyer to be present. Box no. 6210.

 Today we are kittens, but tomorrow we are tigers.
Confused zoologist (F, 34). Box no. 0539.

 None of these things ad up. Rubbish accountant (M,
48). Box no. 0279.

 This column is neither funny nor entertaining. I
should know. Clown and corporate entertainer (M,
94) seeks filthy woman to 25 with no small degree of
familiarity with Leichner make-up. Box no. 3802.

 I've done my sums and the mean average age of male
advertisers in this column since 1998 is 15. Failed
mathematician (F, 28) hoping to find love with mature
gent to 30 (sorry, boys) for slightly longer than my
current two-week relationship record. Box no. 0992.

I'll spend Valentine's Day giving enemas to constipated goats. I'm not a vet, but I do enjoy volunteer work. Man, 31. Box no. 1869.

 Employed in publishing? Me too. Stay the hell away. Man on the inside seeks woman on the outside who likes milling around hospitals guessing the illnesses of out-patients. 30–35. Leeds. Box no. 3287.

 Depressed, oversensitive, edgy tax inspector (F, 35, 13st. 10lb). Accident waiting to happen at box no. 2780.

 Spirit the bluestones¹ of Stonehenge back to Pembrokeshire's glorious Preseli mountains with part-time Carreg Glas archaeological terrorist (full-time on-board caterer for Baltic cruise ships, M, 43). What we miss out in direct action, we make up for in impotent revenge fantasies. Welsh-speaking, bitter females to 50 used to confined quarters and restricted movement write to box no. 9532.

 My lounge is like a disco; my kitchen is like the cocktail bar of a yacht. My garage is like an art museum, but my bedroom is like the Batcave. That's because at night I prowl the city, fighting crime and ridding the streets of evil. Multimillionaire cunningly

---

1   Bluestone: various types of igneous rocks including dolerites, rhyolites and volcanic ash. The bluestones at Stonehenge are thought to have originated from the Preseli hills in Pembrokeshire, the method of their transportation to the site at Stonehenge being the subject of years of speculation.

disguised as mid-thirties IT exec. from Stepney,
still living at mum's. Either it's a dippy egg or that
aeroplane doesn't get anywhere near Mouthy Airport
at box no. 2170.

 To some, I am a world of temptation. To others, I'm
just another cross-dressing pharmacist. M, 41. Box no.
3661.

 Many are called, few are chosen. Telemarketeer (M,
25) wondering where it all went wrong and when can
I get my money back (thanks for nothing, UCL). Box
no. 2387.

 The first thing this column teaches you is not to
struggle. The more you try to break away the tighter
those knots become. If you can, make Silence your
friend. Sure, laughter will help pass many a lonely
hour, but the Silence always returns. Faithful.
Steadying. And when you stare into that darkness, let
Silence embrace you as you yourself embrace the last
forgotten rumours of your life. Drink is a mistress who
will always love you. And I have loved her in return,
drinking of her sweet, fragrant lies – letting her soft
whispers of affection stream through my blood. But
when she is gone, Silence returns and we hold each
other like lovers reconciled after damnable affairs.
Hold me, oh Silence. Keep me close to thy heart that
I may find succour in thy hating breast. Children's
entertainer (M, 56) WLTM nubile F to 25 for sharing of
the lunch bill and tours of the north-west party circuit

(your tasks will include loading the van and inflating balloons). Box no. 2507.

 Blowzy, mousy, and my hair is always lousy
– standard F publishing exec. (36). Does what it says on someone else's tin. Box no. 8754.

 I am not an accountant. Box no. 7542.

 146 is not only my IQ but also my waist size in centimetres. Lecturer in advanced maths and Mensa bore, 51. Bit of a porker but willing to low-carb for at least a fortnight for the right woman (pastry chef and trigonometry fetishist to 50). Box no. 1380.

 My calculator is scientific, my set square is sound. They both tell me that all the angles in my house are out and it's driving me crazy. That's why I've spent the last 24 years of my adult life tearing out the skirting and ripping down partitions. But now I'm finally ready for love. If your doors hang properly, and you know how to steady a spirit level, why not write to obsessive, over-anxious, debarred architect (M, 42)? The windows don't rattle on my house because I've had them all bricked up. Box no. 3679.

 Don't reply to this ad if you are now or have ever been a TA[2] reservist. Orienteering is neither big nor clever, and no one in your department at work ever

---

2   Territorial Army. Part of the British Army made up of reserve units and part-time soldiers. Formed in 1908.

calls you Captain. You know who you are. F, 36. Box no. 5794.

 F, 36, WLTM *LRB*-reading M to 40 who plays darts professionally. Box no. 0189.

 This notice requires you by law to guarantee your love and fidelity for the rest of your life. You can use the form provided, or you could use other Inland Revenue-approved paper versions. Please make sure your missives reach me by 31 January 2004. Otherwise you will have to pay interest, and perhaps a surcharge. Additional forms can be obtained by contacting desperate Civil Service fast-tracker (F, 36). Box no. 3797.

 These ads are all very funny now. But will they be funny in two months' time when you've missed your period? Comprehensive-school sex educationalist (F, 57) seeks man for relationship based on knowing grimaces, OHPs of bearded men, and front-of-class demonstrations involving cucumbers. Syphilis isn't a town in Eastern Europe, you know. Box no. 6331.

 Grange Hill[3] **extra (retired),** latterly university lecturer (M, 34) WLTM woman to 35 obsessed enough by

3   British children's television drama. The series, focusing upon a fictional comprehensive school, was created in 1978 by Phil Redmond, who felt that children's TV didn't adequately tackle the issues confronting youth. It was originally devised to be set in Liverpool, but the setting moved to London because BBC production at the time was in-house. Filming moved to Liverpool in 2002 when Redmond's company Mersey TV took over production. The series became famous

'Where are they now?' features to want desperate affair
with peripheral kids' TV actor of the eighties, thereby
giving herself the vague and remote opportunity
of appearing on such a list. It will never happen,
of course – your clutching self-regard could never
outshine my 2.3 seconds stood behind Mr Bronson
as he stomped down the corridor to confront Mrs
McClusky one more time over an apparent slackening
of school protocol. Less hostile, bordering on the
cuddly, with alcohol. Box no. 4169.

 Gruff train conductor (M, 59) abandoned on the
tracks of love. Your ticket is not valid until 9.15, and
you are required to upgrade to the full standard fare.
All I need is a hug and a valid railcard. Reserved
seating only at box no. 0847.

 Tell me your kidney-stone experiences – I'll set
them to music and we'll make us a West End fortune!
Unemployable choreographer and amateur harpist (M,
62) seeks recovering alcoholic with feeble mind. Own
tap shoes an advantage. Box no. 7353.

for its often controversial storylines, which over the years included
heroin addiction, playground knifings, a gay teacher, attempted
suicide, and teacher bullying. Early seasons provoked tabloid outrage
and national boycotts, but Redmond's insistence on issue-led drama
has seen *Grange Hill* cited as a revolution in children's television.
Notable production members of early seasons include script editor
Anthony Minghella, who later won the Academy Award for Best
Director with *The English Patient*.

Had an accident at work that wasn't your fault? My god I love you. Junior lawyer (M, 62) seeks winnable case/easy sex. Box no. 0856.

My mind is a globe of excitement

If I was a chocolate confection, I'd be a Walnut Whip. You, however, would be a Kinder Surprise.[1] I'm all seriousness and constantly overlooked by those who don't know me; you're a bit thin with a complicated toy that gets stuck in the dog's lungs. Unless one of us can change, this relationship is doomed from the outset. For now, however, let's just revel in the absurdity of fondant love and advanced canine respiratory surgery. Box no. 2867.

 They say an army marches on its stomach. Wrong – it marches on its legs. Sometimes it uses tanks or aircraft and other heavy vehicles. And cars. Box no. 2097.

 Today I feel like a hedgehog. But I want to be a fox. Scotswoman, 26. Box no. 7864.

 I want my mummy. Man (37) with far too many issues to go into detail about in this column seeks psychoanalyst/tailor/stevedore. Whitstable. Box no. 0556.

 'They tell me that this is the kind of thing that gets hold of suburban dwellers once in a while. But most of them just lie down till the feeling passes.' LRB personal ads are the new *Deliverance* and, Honey, I'm

1   Hollow chocolate egg containing a plastic toy (often self-assembly). Originated in Italy in 1974 and available worldwide with the exception of the US, where the toy item is banned by the Food and Drug Administration because of regulations against non-food items being contained within food casing. In the US, the eggs are available with small candies replacing the toy.

their Burt Reynolds (though, admittedly, only during his *Smokey and the Bandit* phase). Looks like we got us a convoy at box no. 8532.

 A tear rolled down his cheek. 'Know him? I *was* that old soldier.' Implausible old loon (56, mad as teeth). 'Bullets were flying above our heads, yet we managed to carry him to safety.' You can call me uncle. Box no. 5286.

 Man, 32, writes poetry like Evel Knievel[2] jumps canyons. Watch me fly at box no. 3698.

 'I never spent much time in school, but I've taught ladies plenty...' Literary Fall Guy[3] of the Tyne (M, 43, I'm the unknown stuntman that made Julian Barnes such a star). Saloon doors in the kitchen and an unfeasible amount of bubbles in the bath. WLTM Heather Locklear-type for nights of winding up in the hay – a hay, hay. Box no. 8646.

 My mind is a globe of excitement. My heart is an atlas of generosity. My body is a map of struggle. You can camp out on the flat heaths, but careful where

2   Robert Craig 'Evel' Knievel (b. 1938, Montana). Stuntman famed for his public displays of motorcycle daring. One-time holder of the world record for number of broken bones. See Appendix.

3   American television series starring Lee Majors playing a stuntman who moonlights as a bounty hunter. The programme's theme song, 'The Unknown Stuntman', was performed by Majors and included the lyric 'I'm the unknown stuntman that made Eastwood such a star'. The ad cites images from the show's opening credits, but it was actress Heather Thomas who appeared alongside Majors in the series and not Heather Locklear.

you tread and remember to close all gates behind you. Akela[4] of desire (F, 38) seeks orienteering M to 45 for nights of bluster and queuing for the showers at box no. 2196.

 Emmdee-Emmay:[5] to you it means nothing but to me it opens the door to wealth beyond your wildest imaginings in the form of a herbal tablet found in my son's wallet that transforms an ageing, withered man (64) into an Asian dancing beauty with tremendous breasts! Patent (and bail) pending. Look at my fingers! They're moving like wondrous vipers! Box no. 4273.

 Am I alone in wanting to concrete over the Lake District? Multiple-level parking enthusiast/NCP[6] eroticist (M, 34, familiar with most forms of therapy) WLTM city-dwelling F ready for night-time random aggregate-dumping campaign and coarse-sand compound repointing. Bring a shovel and expert knowledge of automated ticket-machines to box no. 2826.

 Need more than just a sympathetic ear? I give you the sympathetic leg. For a limited period only, Norwich inventor (M, 34) offers LRB readers the chance to sample the unique 'Leg of Troubles'. Simply whisper what ails ye into the patented Leg Worry

---

4   Leader of cub-scout troops and outward-bound groups.

5   The advertiser is referring phonetically to MDMA, or ecstasy, a drug of the phenethylamine family affecting the release of serotonin in the brain and leading to feelings of euphoria.

6   National Car Parks.

Trumpet and watch all your anxieties of modern living fade away. Send £10 (cash only) and a picture of yourself naked to box no. 2896. Available in teak.

 None of the above? Come fly with me, amateur paraglider on love's flattest heath (M, 104). All we need is a strong head wind and a couple of sturdy helmets. And maybe an ambulance on stand-by. Box no. 6327.

 The best composers are from the Rhineland – Beethoven; Ruyle; Hildegard; Schnorbitz[7] – and so are the best kit-car racers. Join me, darling of the Ahr valley, demon of the Nürburgring racing circuit (leather-clad peroxide F, 57, childless but not joyless), for evenings of stick-shift classical madness and baroque carburettor ballet – in the morning we take on the municipal councils and their inadequate joint regional road-planning extension schemes. It'll be 50 km.p.h., and it'll be the time of your life. Shake your pagoda tree, and hand me that motoring atlas, at box no. 0286.

 My ad comes in the medium of whistles: ppffftttt, ssshhhhhhhwwwwt, peeffwt, pfftpt. Man, 36. Bad at whistling. Box no. 2621.

7   Not a composer but, rather, a St Bernard dog owned by British comedian Bernie Winters, hence the allusion in the ad to *Shake a Pagoda Tree*, the title of the biography of brothers Mike and Bernie Winters.

Pimp My *LRB*! My subscription has chrome rims, neon waterfall lighting, and the baddest, phattest exhaust this side of Osterley. Once inside, however, it's the same old Austin Maxi it's always been – unpredictable, sticky brake pedal, worn clutch, and chipped walnut-veneer dash. M, 51, wants woman with a scooter. May accept all-zone train pass as long as you don't mind my stopping off at the Well-Man clinic along the way (first Tuesday of every month). Box no. 2146.

 I know every boating regulation. And I've broken most of them. Skipper at the helm of uncharted desire (mostly involving a rudder, 6 metres of fishing yarn and a box of docile maggots) seeks first mate for landlocked evenings re-enacting the destruction of the *Hesperus*. Must have own hammock and wellies. M (52), Coventry. Box no. 7343.

 If I were a type of shrub I'd be euonymus. Go figure. Euonymus-esque woman (37). Box no. 7292.

 Let post-Revolutionary disillusionist crush your banditos of doubt with the best vodka jelly this side of Islington. Whatever any of that means. M, 36. Box no. 1449.

 They call me Mr Boombastic.[8] You can call me Monty. My real name, however, is Quentin. But only Mother

---

8 'Boombastic': single released by Shaggy, 1995. Reached number one in the UK charts.

uses that. And Nanny. Monty is fine, though. Anything but Peg Leg (Shrewsbury Prep, 1956, 'Please don't make me do cross-country, sir'). Box no. 0473.

 The difficult follow-up personal ad. Darker lyrics, more keyboards, a four-minute drum solo. In seven years' time you'll hail it as a classic. Until then, make hot and crazy love to me (35-year-old kraut-rocking Innagoddadavida[9] nerd, M). Box no. 7542.

 Put a sock in it! Now two shots of rum. OK, some fresh-squeezed OJ. And some Lego. Surrealist cocktail-maker and barfly guerrilla (M, 35) seeks lady friend to sample the chewiest bloody Marys and the messiest kitchen work-surfaces this side of the Humber. Box no. 7832.

 I am the best-kept secret in Paignton. Box no. 8356.

 Scotch tape. Tippex. Laddered stockings (sheer). Manhattan Transfer[10] and cold nights in the Shropshire wilderness with nothing more than Eça de Queirós[11] to keep us warm. Are you talking my language? Box no. 3036.

---

9 'In-A-Gadda-Da-Vida': Song recorded in 1968 in the spirit of the psychedelic sixties by Iron Butterfly. The song covered one entire side of the album of the same name and, despite being seventeen minutes in length, became a hit in the US.

10 Vocal jazz group formed in 1972.

11 Portuguese writer. Born 1845, died 1900.

The only item you'll find in my fridge is soup. Forty litres of the stuff. Beat that. M, 46. Box no. 7524.

 What I want from you: goose-bumps with your poetic analysis of the seemingly trivial; laughter with your cutting down to size of the overstated; tears at the touch of our hands as we stand watching the waves roll out; shame at your superior knowledge of pre-1972 naval insignia. Perennial deck-hand on love's roughest ocean (M, 47, Fleetwood) seeks Hattie Jacques-at-sea for barrack stanchion shenanigans. It's all grape sigs and grunions bearing drift at box no. 7832.[12]

 This is a terrifying world. I am the only worthy edifice in it. You are probably a tree. You know what I'm saying. Man. 35. Box no. 7213.

 Less Luke Skywalker, more Wedge Antilles[13] (M, 37). Always on the periphery of someone else's story, but reliable and can pilot a TIE Fighter with all boosters a-blazin' (though have nut and shellfish allergy and don't like smokers). Wimbledon. Box no. 5824.

---

12 Deck-hand: ship member who carries out the daily maintenance operations. Hattie Jacques: British comedy actress known for her roles in the Carry On franchise (though none based at sea). Barrack stanchion (naval term): a sailor who rarely goes to sea. Grape sig (naval term): signature given in return for a favour, traditionally given in purple ink. Grunion (naval term): yard worker or, literally, a species of fish.

13 An X-Wing pilot and commander. As a member of the Rebel Alliance, Antilles would never have had the opportunity to pilot a TIE Fighter (Twin Ion Engine), which was, in fact, a space craft used by the Galactic Empire.

Like Dave Eggers,[14] **only better.** Man, 41. Better than Dave Eggers. Box no. 9442.

 During intercourse, I can list Brian Eno's ten favourite books in reverse order. Most women, however, only let me get to number 7 (*Grooming, Gossip and the Evolution of Language* – Robin Fox). M, 34, WLTM woman to 35 willing to let me get to at least number 3 (*The Evolution of Cooperation* – Robert Axelrod). Box no. 8323.

 Are you Kate Bush? Write to obsessive man (36) at box no. 7363. Note: People who aren't Kate Bush need not respond.

 List your five favourite books. First, let me list mine: *The Boy Who Couldn't Stop Washing: The Experience and Treatment of OCD*, Judith L. Rapoport; *Brain Lock: Free Yourself From Obsessive Compulsive Behaviour*, Dr Jeffrey Schwartz; *The Doubting Disease: Help for Scrupulosity and Religious Compulsions*, Joseph W. Ciarrochi; *Imp of the Mind: Exploring the Silent Epidemic of Obsessive Bad Thoughts*, Lee Baer; *The River Café Cookbook*, Rose Gray and Ruth Rogers. F, 32. Enjoys cookery, hairclips, light-switches. Box no. 8313.

 Switching the names on the Sunday Rota Chemist lists of Uttoxeter no longer holds the same thrill it did back in 2002. What I need now is a woman. That's where you come in. You have two degrees in Maths, look like Bettie Page, are a strong swimmer,

14   American writer and editor.

and like nothing better than standing next to the
rabbit cages in branches of Pets at Home and weeping
disconsolately as horrified children look on. Man, 38.
Very, very alone. Box no. 4297.

 **If I could be anywhere in time right now it would be
17 December 1972.** I have my reasons. Man, 57. Box
no. 1553.

 This ad is a seven. But my last one was a nine. Easy.
M, 32. Box no. 5346.

 **I ate a pencil and three Post-Its whilst writing
this ad.** Oh, and drank a bottle of correcting fluid.
Whhheeeeeeee!!! Man, 33-and-a-quarter. Box no.
2378.

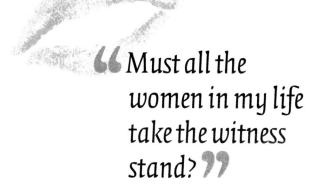

" Must all the women in my life take the witness stand? "

I've experienced some of the finest mace sprays produced in the Western world, but nothing is as painful as placing an ad in here and getting no responses. That's where you come in: blonde, pole-dancing acrobatic F to 21 who isn't put off by two-way mirrors. Man, 82. Box no. 2985.

 Sticks and stones may break my bones but names will never hurt me. Do you find your legal representation inadequate? I once did – in 1992 – but now I'm ready again for love. Write to me, man, 47, Reading. Box no. 8480.

 'Guilty, Your Honour.' Don't let these be my last words ever spoken to a UK resident female. Long-distance offers of love (one letter per month, weight restricted and all contents vetted) to box no. 1673.

 If you get a camcorder for Christmas, can you video-tape your love and send me a copy? If you don't get a camcorder for Christmas, still photos will do. If you don't own a camera, I'll accept donations of cash towards my therapy. Man, 98. Box no. 3286.

 Male *LRB* readers: Luton Expressway is not a gateway to love. You know who you are. So do the authorities. F, 34. Box no. 8342.

 Mah-jong shark of illegal Welsh gambling dens (M, my age is my business) here to reclaim his place as king of the Bloomsbury gamers. Strategic cunning, poker face and all the aces with box no. 7321.

(Respondents should have quick access to a full bank account, a face unrecognisable in Bicester, and be willing to take short-notice long-haul flights.)

 A bottle of fizz, some Howlin' Wolf, a cheap hotel. Add to that my eczema lotion, my prosthetic arm and my probation officer and we may not have the most romantic of evenings but we do have the mother of all poker games. The bets are on with flaking, out-for-the-summer-only M (39), Oxford (and occasionally Pentonville).¹ Box no. 2824.

 Reformed dognapper (M, 43). Box no. 0864.

 Must all the women in my life take the witness stand? Serial embezzler, gangster, fly-tipper and – crucially for the prosecution against an otherwise watertight defence – bigamist (M, 48) WLTM easygoing, dizzy fems to 50 who don't ask too many questions (it's a business trip – I'll be back Tuesday week). Box no. 3663.

 I started advertising in here with the best intentions. Now I find myself on a witness protection programme. Thanks for nothing, LRB. Also Jimmy 'Knuckles' Malone (I thought you were a classics lecturer being ironic). F, 42. New identity, new location, every first Tuesday of the month. Seeks M to 45 with no ties, no traceable numbers, and a hell of

---

1   HM Prison Pentonville, Caledonian Road, London N7.

a lot of petrol in his tank. Non-smokers, non-mafia only. Box no. 9727.

 I know more languages than the advertiser above.
And I've been to jail fewer times. In his favour, I guess his mother doesn't make his lovers sign a guestbook on their way out but two out of three ain't bad, to quote both Meatloaf and my solicitor. Man, 45. Box no. 5279.

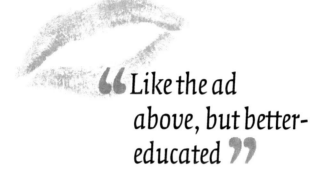

"Like the ad above, but better-educated"

English lecturer. M, 49. It's not all Bachman-Turner Overdrive.[1] But a good portion of it is. Box no. 2642.

 My only academic achievement was contaminating the water supply in class 2C by sneezing over the beaker tray. It caused the biggest outbreak of conjunctivitis ever known at Sutton Primary. I wasn't sorry then and I'm not sorry now. Bitter PR exec. (F, 34) WLTM man to 40 who enjoys living on the edge (of Putney). Box no. 8370.

 The footballing genius of John Sutherland,[2] the academic prowess of Wayne Rooney: if you think I'm screwed up you should see my wardrobe. Queer eye for a straight guy (or mid-forties coaching expert with breasts and a doctorate) sought at box no. 6279.

 Not all female librarians are gay and called Susan. I, however, am and would like to meet non-librarian gay women to 35 with names such as Polly, Kate or Demeter. Chichester. Box no. 5208.

 University lecturer in Russian Literature (male, 57). Great legs. Box no. 1344.

 If you want to, I'll change the situation. Right people, right time, but the wrong location. Dennis Waterman of UCL's darkest corridors seeks

---

1 Canadian rock group formed in 1973. Hits include 'You Ain't Seen Nothin' Yet', which reached number two in the UK charts in 1974.

2 See p. 71, n. 1 and p. 124, n. 11.

Renaissance Studies' own Rula Lenska for crazy East
London gang-related shenanigans. I could be so good
for you at box no. 2290. ³

 Lecturer in Contemporary Dance (M, 47), but you
might remember me as the frontman of the only UK
touring Spanish doo-wop combo of 1982 (Catalan-
A-Ding-Dong; we reached number 104 June that year
with Uma Floridablanca). Catch my rehashed revival
act, Franco-Shoop-Shoop, at all fringe festivals this
summer, but mostly at box no. 5437.

 Brunhilde of Stockport, desperately waiting for hunky
bloke to 40 to pull her from ignominious fire of full-
time lecturing. Must have some understanding of
the vagaries of womanhood and the engines of S-reg
Polos. Box no. 2902.

 **My list of top 100 intellectuals begins and ends
with Bernie Clifton.**⁴ If you have a fake ostrich and a
slim-jim tie, you could shoehorn yourself in there and
gain a place in my heart to boot. Radical biologist/
slapstick comedian (M, 57). Box no. 8552.

3   The advertiser is referring to the popular British television series
Minder, which ran from 1979 to 1994 and starred Dennis Waterman
as Terry McCann alongside George Cole as Arthur Daley, a wheeler-
dealer figure with low scruples. The show's theme tune, 'I Could Be
So Good for You', was performed by Waterman and included lines
cited in the advert. It reached number three in the UK charts in 1980.
Waterman married Rula Lenska in 1987. They divorced in 1998.

4   St Helens (Merseyside) comedian famed for riding a fake ostrich
on stage.

Sure, I could spend all day trying to shoehorn Slavoj Žižek[5] into a personal ad, but when we finally get to meet I'm going to spend the whole time just staring at your breasts. No illusions at box no. 9623.

 I never got a chance to see him, never heard nutin' but bad things about him. Momma, I'm depending on you (funk-laden, trippy woman with soul, 40–45) to tell me the truth. Papa was a lecturer in Renaissance Studies at box no. 5576.[6]

 Finished with my woman 'cos she couldn't help me with my mind. Midlands M, 46. Wanted Lacan, got Black Sabbath. And that, Adam Phillips, is analysis.[7] Box no. 8379.

 Child prodigy and Slade genius (M, 52). Leonine looks, condescending only when the moment demands it, and prone to bouts of severe creativity. Catch me now – in the corridors of the Carré d'Art, slightly past my peak – before tuberculosis, pleurisy or Brian Sewell creeps in. The absinthe is on me at box no. 8334.

5   Slovenian cultural critic and author.

6   'Papa Was a Rollin' Stone': single released by the Undisputed Truth in 1972, reaching number sixty-three in the US charts. Later a number-one hit for the Temptations and winner of three Grammy Awards in 1973.

7   The lyrics quoted here are taken from 'Paranoid', a single released by Black Sabbath in 1970. Jacques Lacan: French psychoanalyst whose work influenced many fields including linguistics and critical theory. Adam Phillips: psychotherapist, essayist and author.

Chippy little maths teacher (in a mental-breakdown sort of way). Male, 43, you know the shirt and the hair already. WLTM flamboyant drama-type F for irritating discussions about the value of science over art, then strip Cluedo. It's Reverend Green in the lounge with the spanner; now let's make love like pussycats. Box no. 7286.

 Resident Flemish biologist typical in a North West family (consisting also of mother, father, overbearing grandparent and fourteen siblings). Would like to hear from women in similar situation. Box no. 0544.

 I like you because you read magazines with big words. And you've got great booblies. I can live without the first. But the second is non-negotiable. Shallow man, 34. When I say 'shallow', I mean, damn. Box no. 7742.

 If his status ain't hood I ain't checking fo' him. Classics lecturer (F, 53), wishes she had Beyoncé's stomach, bling and movement. Though not necessarily her appreciation of lyric poetry. I want a soldier, or else any sane man within M25, at box no. 9521.[8]

 Module 1: provide evidence to show that you have read a literary magazine; provide evidence to show that you have experience of setting up a direct debit; provide evidence to show that you have spent considerable

---

8   The ad refers to the song 'Soldier', by Destiny's Child, whose line-up includes the singer Beyoncé Knowles.

time alone and don't look likely ever to have sex again without spending some serious money and/or changing your pants (M, 32). Awaiting the results of my NVQ in Desperation at box no. 3111.

 I use this column principally as a sounding board for my radical philosophical theories. This time, however, I'd like some sexual intercourse. Radical philosopher and occasional lust monkey. M, 41. Box no. 4088.

 Like the ad above, but better educated and well-read. Also larger bosoms. Man, 38, Watford. Box no. 2712.

 Call for papers: '*London Review of Books* personal ads: an exaggeration or a rejection of the dominant cultural norm?' Send proposal to gay, anorexic, flamenco-dancing M, 36, baby-blue eyes, blond hair, and pesto recipes to die for. Box no. 1369.

 ***LRB* readers.** You are all just English lecturers who like Björk.[9] Get over it, then make love to me. Each and every damn one of you. Man, 98, Berks. Box no. 3752.

 Stroganoff. Boysenberry, Frangipani. Words with their origins in people's names. If your name has produced its own entry in the OED then I'll make love to you. If it hasn't, I probably will anyway, but I'll only want you for your body. Man of too few distractions, 32. Box no. 2576.

---

9 Singer/songwriter, formerly lead singer with the Sugarcubes.

What is your favourite preserved body part? Mine is the diseased bladder of Italian biologist Lazzaro Spallanzani[10] (currently on display in the Scarpa Room in the University of Pavia). This and many more conversation killers available from librarian and failed travel agent, F, 32, Northampton. Box no. 4279.

 OMG! This magazine is the shizz. Seriously, dudes. Awesome! LOL! Classics lecturer (M, 48). Possibly out of his depth with today's youth. KTHX! Box no. 2680.

 If John Sutherland were a soul disco diva, would he sing Barry White?[11] Hopeful author of new OUP modern philosophy series (read my pilot, 'Who would win in a fight between Proust and Marvin Gaye?'). Man, 37, WLTM woman to 40 who would be *Wuthering Heights* read by Rose Royce if she were a 19th-century novel given to a '70s supergroup. Box no. 3579.

10   Italian biologist (b. 10 January 1729, d. 12 February 1799) whose work on the theory of the spontaneous generation of cellular life proved that microbes come from the air and can be killed through boiling. He also proved that animal reproduction requires both sperm and ovum and was the first to perform an artificial insemination (a dog was used). His most renowned body of work, however, was the *Dissertationi de fiscia animale e vegetale* (1780), in which he proved that the process of digestion is one not simply of trituration but of chemical solution produced by the action of gastric fluids.

11   See p. 71, n. 1 and p. 119, n. 2. The advertiser is here referring to Sutherland's publications *Is Heathcliff a Murderer? Puzzles in Nineteenth-Century Fiction; Can Jane Eyre Be Happy? More Puzzles in Classic Fiction; Who Betrays Elizabeth Bennet? Further Puzzles in Classic Fiction* and *Henry V, War Criminal? and Other Shakespeare Puzzles* (with Cedric Watts). All books originally published by Oxford University Press.

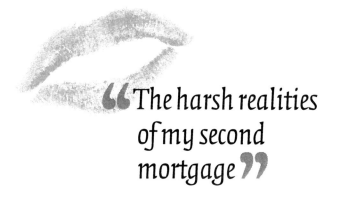

"The harsh realities of my second mortgage"

I've got money to burn! Also my receipts for the last eight financial years, but that's another story. Pensive man, 36, seeks diligent lawyer/lover/chef/priest/whatever. Box no. 2821.

 Your clothes are all made by Balmain, and there's diamonds and pearls in your hair.[1] My clothes are all Next red-dot jobs, and I'm completely bald. Think about the possibilities. Can you lend me a tenner? Yes you can, yes you can. Man, 35. Box no. 8532.

 Ladies: apply now for opportunity to make love with Roman gladiator (bankrupt publisher, 5′2″, but every bit a man). Box no. 5890.

 Junoesque, blonde, 52-year-old provocative sex moggy (still with own fur, fully inoculated and house-trained) seeks similar male to scratch under her chin at night. Must be able to write own name (on own cheque book a bonus). Previous applicants need not apply. Box no. 4069.

 Bastard son of Dean Friedman. Do you still love me? Are you still angry? Are you between 45 and 55 with a healthy portfolio of stocks and shares? Then write to bearded freak at box no. 6290.[2]

---

1 The advertiser is referring to the song 'Where Do You Go To (My Lovely)', single released by Peter Sarstedt in 1969 (reached number four in the UK charts and won the Ivor Novello Award).

2 The advertiser is referring to both 'Lucky Stars', sung by Dean Friedman and Denise Marsa, a top-ten UK hit in 1978, and 'Bastard Son of Dean Friedman', sung by Birkenhead band Half Man Half Biscuit (1986).

I'm square E4 on page 43 of the London mini *A–Z*
(colour edition). I really need you (M, to 40, solvent,
slightly awkward but appreciative of the opportunity
for a regular sex life after all these years) to be in E3,
page 49. Over-mortgaged F, 35. Box no. 3027.

 Your place or your other place? Woman, 32, needful
of the finer things in life seeks stinking-rich bloke,
80 to 100. Must be willing to fibrillate his ventricles
when he becomes tiresome or bankrupt or both. Also
interesting thirty-somethings for illicit and immoral
affair to be conducted concurrently with the above.
Box no. 1597.

 Less-than-successful gambler and author of niche,
print-on-demand business titles (American, M, 55)
WLTM attractive, docile UK woman, willing to pay
up-front for 312 copies of *Synergy or Competition:
Distribution and Dissemination of Financial Reports to
Non-Financial Company Middle-Management Tiers in the
Terrifying New Dawn of Interdepartmental Co-operation or
Everything You Wanted to Know about Non-Accountable
Revenue Channels but Were Too Afraid to Ask (Volume 3)*.
Must know how to calm a hysterical and broken man
with only the next race to live for (but I've got a great
tip from Ed in the bar – it's a sure thing, honey). Box
no. 5275.

 God appeared to me in a dream last night and spoke
your name in my ear. He gave me the winning lottery
numbers, too, though, so you can understand where
my priorities lay when I raced to grab a notebook

and pen. Man, 37, living on hope and the next seven
weeks' bonus balls seeks woman whose first name
begins with S, or maybe F, and rhymes with chicken,
and has a surname that's either a place in Shropshire
or the title of a 1979 Earth, Wind and Fire track.
Shicken Boogiewonderland, I know you're reading
this. Write now to box no. 5279.

 Credit-card debt? Bills getting on top of you?
Reminders arriving daily through your letterbox?
Consolidate your debt into one convenient loan,
then write to dodgy-endowment-selling M, 37,
Bedfordshire, at box no. 3753. CCJs, mortgage
arrears, refused past credit, all accepted. Your home is
at risk if you do not keep up repayments.

 Reply to this advert, then together we can face the
harsh realities of my second mortgage. M, 38, WLTM
woman to 70 with active credit cards. Box no. 8624.

 **If you don't open the letters from the credit-card
company**, it's just like they never asked for their
money back. Woman, 36, would like to hear from
any men (professionals, blond, to 45) for whom this
defence has worked in an actual court of law. Box no.
1780.

 You'll write; I'll probably enjoy your letter and write
back. After corresponding a few times, several phone
calls, we'll arrange to meet. We'll meet again and
become more intimate, eventually dating regularly.
We'll form a relationship, start leaving things at each

other's apartments. We'll spend weekends together.
Sometimes whole weeks. We'll have lazy Sundays lying
naked in bed together, reading the supplements and
not leaving the house. Sometimes we'll disagree. The
disagreements will become rows. We'll see each other
less in the week. You'll come around one evening to
'collect some things' – we both know what it means.
You'll go back to your place and cry like you used
to do on cold, wintry evenings. I'll drink more and
cultivate a fetish for Kirsty Wark trouser suits.[3] We'll
regret six lost months – possibly a year – wasted on yet
another emotional cul-de-sac. Let's save us both the
pain – just send me a Christmas card and a nice gift
(cash preferred, donations of £20 and above) and we'll
call the whole thing quits now. Insolvent bookie and
amateur psychotherapist (M, 43). Box no. 4782.

3   Kirsty Wark (Aquarius): presenter of BBC's *Newsnight*.

"This column reads
like a list of
X-File character
rejects"

Cut out the headlines from every essay in this edition of the *LRB*. Remove each occurrence of the letter O. Now rearrange the remaining letters into groups of vowels and consonants. Add up the number in each group. Now multiply those numbers by the nearest higher prime number to each. Divide the numbers you're left with by the number of the page in this issue on which the word 'station' first appears. Write both of those numbers on separate pieces of paper, with the word 'Mesmer' written in pencil beneath each. Now dig a hole in your garden exactly 11 feet deep and put those pieces of paper in it. Fill the hole back up and return to it at the end of June, which just happens to be the sixth month of the year. Coincidence? I think not. M, 57. Box no. 6138.

 In the year 2273, dogs will walk on their hind legs and eat at tables with men. The tables will float in the air, propelled by some sort of anti-gravitational force – assuming there'll still be gravity. Which I doubt very much, because in the year 2128, fish-like creatures will invade the earth and drink its gravity like hot soup. But tomorrow you and I (M, 32) will love each other, and caress our hair like the gentle Koala-Men of Graaaxxux-9.[1] Box no. 1302.

 This column is a ziggurat of heartache and I am its High Priest. Pork Belly-Eating Champion, Stroud, 1981 (M, 47). Box no. 8821.

---

1 Does not exist.

Leading a ragtag fugitive fleet on a lonely quest for a shiny planet known as Earth. [2] Join me – I may want to meet more of your kind. Ridiculous M still dependent on his mother after all these years (43 of them). Make sure it's a chucky egg or I won't eat it. For centuries we have travelled, etc., etc. Box no. 6231.

 Using advanced quantum mechanics and some bits from an old Breville sandwich toaster, I have been to the future and witnessed its glories. They say men will never be able to hover like wasps, but I tell you they haven't witnessed our many bounteous unions with the delightful Wasp People of Ruislip's as yet undiscovered subterranean caverns. Join me, and let us be the first to offer up our bodies and secure majestic wasp-like hovering abilities for generations to come. Man, 63. Possibly ingesting medicines that shouldn't be taken orally. Box no. 2268.

 Open your heart to the impossible! One day, men will possess psychic tentacles capable of reading the minds of our lovers and satisfying their every desire. Until then, you'll just have to put up with accident-prone biological researcher (M, 35). I'm all fingers, thumbs, and whatever the hell this thing growing on my elbow is. Box no. 8545.

---

2   The advertiser is alluding to *Battlestar Galactica*, an American television series that began with a three-hour pilot aired in 1978 and starred Lorne Greene, Richard Hatch and Dirk Benedict as part of the crew of a battleship of near-extinct humans in search of a fabled planet called Earth.

A chicken laid an egg. And when that egg hatched a chick appeared. That chick grew up and in its turn laid an egg. When that egg hatched, sure enough a chick appeared and fed and grew and in its turn laid an egg. The egg hatched. And the chick that hatched from that egg fed and grew and loved and laid an egg. But when that egg hatched, they found this ad inside! 42-year-old chemical-ingesting loon (M). Box no. 4731.

 This advert is the thinnest in the paper. As such, it offers little burning potential should a disaster strike the earth and fuel become unavailable to those other than the most powerful. Burn the other ads instead, and sleep with mine under your pillow, dreaming of what might have been had you actually replied to it rather than making contingency plans for the end of the world. Woman, 39, seeks man to 45 who isn't prone to bouts of panic buying or nervous rashes. Box no. 0886.

 'Regarding the cerebellum, there is a culture and a presentation. Both hold sway.' *Andromeda*-fixated[3] thirty-something poof. Damn sure I'm not the only one in here. Fairly certain, however, that I do have the finest frontal lobes in the tri-galaxies and would look hot as fusion in a bikini. Please help me. Box no. 5553.

 When American scientists tried to forge ahead in the space race by adapting the alien technologies they had recovered from the crashes in the Nevada desert

3 *Andromeda*: American science-fiction television series.

during the fifties, they overlooked me. That's because
I'm not a scientist, know nothing about spacecraft
or alien technology and come from Burnley. In other
respects, I was the ideal man for the job. You may want
to consider this when looking for a well-groomed,
articulate, handsome, educated late-twenties blond
gentleman. Man, 45, beard. Box no. 6421.

 I have a recipe for space cakes. My theory is that,
when they're eaten, the human body no longer needs
oxygen to survive for as long as the cakes are being
digested. The key ingredient is a derivative of a plant
used by inhabitants of the Pacific islands thousands
of years ago that enabled them to dive for extended
periods whilst fishing. Once made stable, this
ingredient lasts longer in the human body, making
longer, less cumbersome space-walks possible.
What I currently lack, however, is the money to
make this venture happen. That's where you come
in: big-chested 21-year-old rich totty with fondness
for 62-year-old loons. Write quickly – time, and the
nurses, are against me. Box no. 2133.

 The body of Salman Rushdie, but the head of Gerald
Kaufman; like some horrific Kurt Neumann film.[4] But

4 Salman Rushdie: author. Gerald Kaufman: Labour Member of
Parliament. Kurt Neumann: director of the 1958 horror classic *The
Fly*, in which a scientist experimenting with a teleportation device
accidentally merges his molecular structure with that of a fly trapped
in his machine. Gerald Kaufman was first mentioned in the LRB
personals in 1999 after chairing that year's Booker Prize. His name
was mentioned in many ads over the course of the next two years,
earning a cult-like status among personal advertisers for no apparent
reason whatsoever.

don't think I want your pity (just practical help and loving.) Box no. 1576.

 Trendy Zoroastric nancy-boy (35) seeks non-pantheistic cohort to 45 to help prepare for the mighty battle against Angra Manyu.[5] Must like coffee bars and Alan Bennett. Northampton. Box no. 4789.

 You may call it indecent exposure, but I call it the divine hand of God. Spiritualist of the Asda car-park (acquitted) seeks docile woman for easy brainwashing and to help bring the tinned stuff home. Must have own trolley and strong arms. Beds. Box no. 3696.

 '92 – a retired physician/ He couldn't know about his future ignition' – Fortean poet currently on the path to the world's first SHC epic – 'For almost a century he'd been a fighter/ Now a human cigarette lighter.'[6] Publishers, or desperate women, please

5 In Zoroastrianism, Angra Manyu is the ruler of the forces of evil.

6 The advertiser is thought to be referring to Dr John Irving Bentley, who died in mysterious circumstances aged ninety-two at his home in Coudersport, Pennsylvania, on 5 December 1966. Don Gosnell, a meter-reader from the North Penn Gas Co., had been doing his daily rounds and called at Bentley's home on North Main Street. While reading the meter in the basement, Gosnell noticed a strange smell and a peculiar blue smoke. He went upstairs to investigate and found Bentley's cremated remains in the bathroom. The lower half of Bentley's right leg was all of his body that remained intact, yet the rubber tips on his walking frame hadn't been damaged and there was very little scorching on the nearby bathtub. Indeed, apart from a hole burned through the linoleum floor, there was very little fire damage to the bathroom at all. The coroner recorded a verdict of 'death by asphyxiation and 90 per cent burning of the body'. The story of Dr Bentley is one of the most documented cases of spontaneous human combustion (SHC), which is a theory applied to instances of

write to stigmatic man, 36, with uncanny powers of bi-location and the ability to bend raining frogs. Anti-gravitational love, and full back-catalogue of Orbis Publications' *The Unexplained*⁷ (issue 2 free with issue 1), from box no. 4459.

 Chew your food. It's better for your digestion and improves the facial muscles. Also it breaks up the signals from the taps government agents place inside potato-based products. Want more tips? Write to South West man (41) with big heart and untraceable phone-line. Box no. 7431.

 'All he needs are some psychiatric treatments to reduce the strength and regularity of his biorhythmic brain explosion episodes. For one so young, his powers of telekinesis are far beyond that of any project we've developed so far. His brain has the power to rule the world. It may cause you some problems at home, but the benefits of the bionic mind far outweigh the pitfalls.' My school report, 1979 (Porton Down Preparatory School).⁸ So much promise then, look at me now. Ex-superhero, now librarian (M, 31) seeks solvent woman to 35 for Scrabble, real ale and spontaneous morphing. Wilts. Box no. 1179.

death where a person has seemingly caught fire without any obvious explanation.

7 Partwork magazine focusing on the paranormal and published by Orbis in 1982. Re-issued regularly since then.

8 Porton Down, in Wiltshire, is home to the Porton Down Defence Science and Technology Laboratory, a facility for military, chemical and biological weapons research.

The *LRB*'s own Son of Jor-El, stuck in the Phantom Zone of the personal ads for three years now.⁹ Reckon I could still lick anyone of you wusses. Man, 36. Alone. Tonight, and very possibly for ever. Box no. 4723.

 This column reads like a list of X-File character rejects. Woman, 34, able to bi-locate and start fires with the power of her pre-menstrual tension. Seeks human/Jovian hybrid with whom to start genetic processing plant (Bicester). Must have own car. Box no. 5258.

 'If you can't take a little bloody nose, maybe you oughtta go back home and crawl under your bed. It's not safe out here. It's wondrous, with treasures to satiate desires both subtle and gross; but it's not for the timid.'¹⁰ LRB personals are the Next Generation. Serial advertiser (M, 37) knows it but still comes back for more (and more). Please help me. Box no. 6311.

 With enough love I can teleport like Mary of Agreda.¹¹ That's got to be worth something here,

9 Jor-El is the biological father of Superman. The Phantom Zone is a fictional dimension in the *Superman* comics that is used as a method of imprisonment. From here, prisoners can observe the normal dimension but cannot interact with it.

10 The advertiser is quoting an episode of *Star Trek: The Next Generation*, an American science-fiction television series continuing the *Star Trek* franchise.

11 Maria de Agreda, also known as Maria de Jesus or the Blue Nun. Born in 1602, she is believed to have endured ecstasies and divine visions from an early age. Four years after her death, Franciscans reported that, whilst alive, at twenty-two she had been mystically transported to Mexico to convert indigenous tribes and had

right? Right? Transvective surburbanite (F, 38),
unwittingly adding to the growing list of LRB
Googlewhacks¹² at box no. 8556.

 More Grand Moff Tarkin¹³ than Darth Vader – not
quite evil enough, but working at it M (35) WLTM
gullible F to 40 with whom to annunciate ev-er-y syll-
able whilst taking over the un-i-verse. Join me in my
Tooting Death Star for canapés, intimidating silences,
and perfect posture. Box no. 2306.

 **This ad is the final phase in my plan to conquer the
earth.** Man, 41, seeks puppet-like trillionaire F with
vast army and intergalactic fleet, ready to hand over
total control of all affairs. Must also enjoy canasta and
be a non-smoking vegetarian. Box no. 3510.

 But what the authorities didn't reckon on was
my ability to stop a goat's heart with my mind. Ex-
Master Criminal and Super Villain (F, 42), now Dorset
museum curator, WLTM bald, wheelchair-bound,
telekinetic biophysicist with morphing powers to
relive old times thwarting the do-good citizens of
Weymouth. For tomorrow we take on the world. Box
no. 1379.

subsequently made five hundred journeys through the air for the same
purpose in just one year.

12   Googlewhack: internet search term consisting of two words
(without quotation marks) that yields a single result. When this
ad was originally published, it was indeed a Googlewhack. Now,
however, the search term yields no results.

13   Commander of the Death Star, the Galactic Empire's ultimate
terror weapon.

Attention male *LRB* readers: 'Greetings, Earthling – I have come to infest your puny body with legions of my spawn' is no way to begin a reply. F, 36 – suspicious of any men declaring themselves to be in possession of a 'great sense of humour'. Box no. 6413.

 Whenever I try to cancel my *LRB* subscription, I suffer stigmata and holy visions dance around my bedroom like so many drunken midgets. Man, 41, Leicester. Possibly the Messiah, or something. Box no. 6108.

"Failure? Pah!
I invented the
word**"**

The most used button on my keyboard is the underscore. I haven't used it once in the making of this ad. I don't know what that says about my personality, but I'm fairly confident it isn't good. Woman, 32. Box no. 8653.

 I used to have the sharpest mind in the land; now I can't even find my pen. Wait – here it is! Pens, and offers of sex, please, to retired professor (M, 71). Box no. 8308.

 I used to be exactly 29 days ahead of my time. I've just wasted all that writing this ad. Currently I stand at just 3 hours. I'll spend that regretting not having stamps. Box no. 6354.

 This personal ad is in excellent condition when packed. When used however, it may be found to contain some crystals. These crystals are common salt and are perfectly harmless. The condiment of love demands your Pot Noodle;[1] the fork of reason your reconstituted soya. Loser (M, 33) fishing out all the dried peas before the kettle is boiled at box no. 3621.

 But it was all over at the main course, when the lobster made his neck enlarge and the waiter had to perform a tracheotomy with the dessert spoon. After that, any sort of physical love was out of the question. Yet we remained good (if largely silent) friends. Sound

---

1   Reconstituted noodle and vegetable ramen-style snack available in the UK. Popular with students and people whose only cooking facility is a kettle.

familiar? Stop me if I'm wrong, but I think this girl
(buxom, 51, all woman) is talking your language.
Don't be afraid – this sort of intimacy is only natural.
Box no. 4721.

 Terrorist Amazon reviewer: '1 star – this book sucks
big time/I've had more fun operating on my own
cataracts/this book is the most entertainment you'll
have providing you use it for smacking geese in your
local park rather than actually reading it.' Sound
familiar, publicity departments of the fourth estate?
M, 43, holed up at home with chicken pox during the
marches of '68, now reinventing anarchy in his own
impotent way. Box no. 6273.

 Married, divorced, married, divorced, but that doesn't
mean there is a pattern developing. Optimistic lad,
mid-fifties, seeks woman, for NE based relationship.
Box no. 8765.

 **It is better to die on your feet than to live on your
knees.** Unless your house has very low ceilings.
In which case, come and view our latest range
of spacious waterfront properties. Tasteful new
developments, modern décor, off-road parking. Ex-
revolutionary, now beaten but unbroken estate agent
(41). I've made better pitches than this, you know. And
had better-looking women than you. Box no. 5643.

 Grave disappointment all round WLTM serious
mistake in a nightie. Box no. 6453.

Failure? Pah! I invented the word. On the same day I also came up with the word 'hoosler' (noun: a person who makes a living screwing caps on to bicycle-wheel inner-tube valves) and followed that up later in the week with 'ledgtentrible' (to describe a downward sloping chin). Only the first really took off. You have to appreciate the irony. Man, 78, bisexual. Box no. 3175.

 Born under a bad sign: 'Skelmersdale next exit'. After that it was a life of emotional service stops and never-ending circuits on North West ring roads. Are you my final Little Chef or an emergency pull-up on the hard shoulder of despair? Man, 32. Cries like a girl and phones his mother a lot. Box no. 5285. Junction 13.

 The uncomfortable mantle of guilt, the heavy cloak of ignominy, the coarse socks of denial, the iridescent trousers of doubt, the belligerent underpants of self-loathing. All worn by the haberdasher of shame (M, 34, Pembs.). Seeks woman in possession of the Easy-Up iron-on hem of redemption and some knowledge of workaday delicates. No loons. Box no. 4635.

 I once trained with the nation's best and most respected architects – now I can't erect a garden shed. Did lust destroy your creative energies too? Great – write immediately to suburban love wretch (M, 39), Tooting Broadway. Box no. 8525.

 Make love to me. Or at the very least buy my car. 5-door Astra, J-reg. Good runner. 8 mnths tax, 10

mnths MOT. 60,000 miles. One careful owner. M,
38, alcoholic, bankrupt, divorced, sleeping in the ex-
wife's Micra. £2,000 ono (sex is extra). Box no. 5342.

 She signed the letter 'All yours, Babooshka'.[2] Little
did I know that Babooshka wasn't, in fact, my wife
trying to catch my infidelity (thanks for nothing, Kate
Bush), but a gorgeous East European minx looking
for no-strings love and a place to rest her tired head
every now and again. If only I'd realised when I replied
with a parcel of my smalls and a request to use non-
bio (I have very sensitive skin). The bad-luck fairy sits
permanently on the shoulders of male doofus (38) at
box no. 3121.

 Sexless, dour and uninteresting – and that was just
my driving-test report. Post-plucking woman (41)
representing a real challenge to the sternest of male
egos seeks cavalryman to 45 ready to throw off this
knitted plaid mantle and cast it into the fires of lusty
abandon. Or else we could just play Jenga. Shropshire
borders. Box no. 2542.

 **Attracting a mate with these ads is like shooting
fish in a barrel.** Blind marksman (M, 38), firing
blanks the wrong way, seeks bigger target fitted with

2 Taken from 'Babooshka', single released by Kate Bush in July 1980.
The song relates the story of a man who is sent a sequence of love-
letters. He falls in love with the writer, reminded by their contents
of his wife in the early days of their relationship 'when she was
beautiful'. The author of the letters is, in fact, his wife who is writing
under the assumed identity of Babooshka in an attempt to prove her
husband's adultery. Reached number five in the UK charts.

klaxon for narrowing of implausible odds. Dulwich.
Box no. 5363.

 If Mother could see me now. Fortunately her bad
hip prevents her coming up the stairs too often. Man,
36, seeks woman to 40 before the stairlift engineers
are called out and my love life has to run its course in
shopping-centre food courts yet again. Box no. 6407.

 'A game hardly worth the candle' (ex-second wife,
Jan. 1997). Box no. 2549.

 **By the time they publish this personal ad you'll
have found someone else.** Two weeks too late
woman (37), always at the mercy of LRB publishing
cycles. Box no. 3542.

 Ladies: naturally apologetic man, 42, predisposed to
accepting the blame. Whatever it was, it was my fault.
Sorry. Sound like heaven? Box no. 5233.

 **One day all these ads will be collected in a huge
best-selling volume** and a question on them will
appear in Oxbridge undergraduate finals. Mine
won't be there, of course. Entirely forgettable man
(43) hoping to find humdrum woman for eventual
long-term disappointment. Replies when you can be
bothered to box no. 2787.

Das echte Dividuum ist auch das echte Individuum.[3]
At least that's what I tell my mother. And her cats.
Please hold me (M, 68). Box no. 7664.

 Don't reply to this ad – it's a fake. Just like the man
who placed it. Deny nothing, regret all, but live to
fight another day with phenomenologically ashamed,
melanin-deprived, testosterone-poisoned scion of the
patriarchal ruling class system (32, Worcester). Box
no. 7590.

 How can I follow that? Man, 47. Gives up easily. Box
no. 9547.

 HOWZAT![4] Ex-Sherbet groupie (mulleted F, 46),
currently lecturer in Fine Arts. The good days aren't
coming back, are they? Please kiss me. Box no. 7958.

 Don't reply to this ad – I'll only end up confessing
that the thing about having a second book deal was a
lie and there is no author tour in the pipeline. Man, 39,
just secured second book deal and about to embark on
author tour. Box no. 8676.

 The room was silent and the tree in the corner still,
its delicate baubles shimmering in the moonlight

3 'The genuine dividual is also the genuine in-dividual.' From *Das
Allgemeine Brouillon* by German author Novalis (1772–1801). Novalis,
together with Friedrich Schlegel, developed a theory of the fragment
as a literary form of art.

4 'Howzat': single released by pop group Sherbet on 25 September
1976. Reached number four in the UK, staying in the charts for ten
weeks.

that crept through the frosted window. Outside and
in the distance he fancied he could hear the jingle of
bells, fading into the Northern Lights. The ground
outside was blanketed thick with fresh, crisp snow. He
would be out there at the rising of the sun, building
snowmen and dressing them with his gloves and
hat, but for the moment there were more important
things to consider in the parlour. Slowly at first, so
as to make the moment last that little bit longer, he
teased the shiny wrapper from the corner of the box,
then, with excited fingers and eyes wide, he stripped it
bare, throwing the paper behind him and tearing the
cardboard lid until he could see its contents peeping
out. Suddenly a darkness fell upon his face. Oh no,
Santa. This isn't right. Why have you let me down
again? Why have you betrayed my trust? All I wanted
was a woman to 40 (preferably within the M25).
'Damn you, Santa!' he cried, flinging open the window
and letting the icy night fly in. 'Damn your very eyes!'
'Are you all right, son?' asked his 64-year-old mother,
whom he had spent most of his adult life caring for,
without any thanks, without any consolation, and
without any willingness on her part even to look
through the care-home brochures. 'Yes,' he sobbed
softly into his sleeve, before looking up through
tearful eyes; 'please hug me, Mummy.' The bells in the
distance had vanished. The sun had started to rise. 'Is
Santa coming back next year?' 'Yes, son, Santa always
comes back for good boys.' Box no. 7966.

 **These ads are a sudden heady rush of pleasure in
an otherwise sterile world (Runcorn).** I have little to

offer other than my willingness to embrace failure and
a clear view of the ICI plant. Man, 45. Box no. 8653.

 **Lacks imagination, talks too much, frequently
absent.** Look at me now, Miss Webster of Year 4.
History professor, 56. Lacks imagination, talks too
much and is frequently absent. Seeks woman. Box no.
8025.

 With Oxford bi-plane modeller (M, 51), patience and
innovation are a daily experience. So too, however, is
gluing my head to my shoulder. Cyanoacrylate,[5] and a
whole lot of lovin', please, to box no. 7990.

 Shake hands with Dalkeith,[6] Midlothian! Official
greeter and face of Dalkeith Cheese Festival, 1974,
seeks woman to 50 who is no stranger to failure,
debt-consolidating mortgages, and wool. Must enjoy
beards and harbour contempt for any music that isn't
Belgian jazz. Box no. 8970.

5   Major component of substances such as methyl-2-cyanoacrylate,
also known as superglue, and the surgical glue 2-octyl cyanoacrylate.
Can be softened by liberal applications of acetone, which is found in
nail-polish remover.

6   'A town and a parish in the East of Edinburghshire. The town
stands 182 feet above sea level on a peninsula from 3 to 5 furlongs
wide, between the North and South Esk's [sic] and by roads 4¼ miles
South by West of Musselburgh, and 6 miles South East of Edinburgh.
The High Street widens Eastwards from 30 to 85 feet, and terminates
at a gateway leading up to Dalkeith Palace, the principal seat of the
Duke of Buccleuch, which palace, has centring round it all the chief
episodes in Dalkeith's history, must here be treated of before Dalkeith
itself.' From *Ordnance Gazeteer of Scotland* 1885.

Evel Knievel
chronology of jumps and injuries

1965 Moses Lake, Washington. *In a stunt to win publicity for his motorcycle dealership, Knievel leaps off a ramp to clear two mountain lions, but lands in a box of rattlesnakes.*

1966 **23 January** – Indio, California: National Date Festival Grounds
10 February – Barstow, California. *Attempts to jump, spread-eagle, over a speeding motorcycle. Jumps too late and is hit in the groin by the motorcycle and tossed fifteen feet into the air. Hospitalised.*
1 June – Post Falls, Idaho: State Line Gardens
19 June – Missoula, Montana: Missoula Auto Track. *Attempts to jump twelve cars and a cargo van. Fails to reach speed required for take-off. Back wheel hits the top of the van and front wheel hits the top of the landing ramp. Suffers severely broken arm and several broken ribs.*
19 August – Great Falls, Montana: Great Falls Speedway
30 October – Butte, Montana: Naranche Memorial Drag Strip

1967 **5 March** – Gardena, California: Ascot Park Speedway
30 May – Gardena, California: Ascot Park Speedway

28 July – Graham, Washington: Graham Speedway. *Tries to clear sixteen cars in a jump. Lands on the last vehicle, a panel truck, and is thrown from the bike. Suffers serious concussion.*

18 August – Graham, Washington: Graham Speedway. *Attempts the same jump as 28 July. Hits the last vehicle again and crashes, breaking left wrist, right knee and two ribs.*

24 September – Monroe, Washington: Evergreen Speedway

23–26 November – San Francisco, California: Civic Center

2 December – Long Beach, California: Long Beach Arena

31 December – Las Vegas, Nevada: Caesar's Palace. *Televised attempt to jump the fountain at Caesar's Palace. Bike unexpectedly decelerates on take-off causing Knievel to land on a safety ramp supported by a van. Loses grip of handlebars and falls over them and on to the pavement, skidding into a parking lot. Suffers crushed pelvis and femur, fractures to hip, wrist and both ankles and a concussion. Lies in a coma for twenty-nine days. Leg is rebuilt with two-foot steel strip.*

1968 **25 May** – Scottsdale, Arizona: Beeline Dragway. *Crashes while attempting to jump fifteen Ford Mustang cars. Breaks right leg and foot.*

3 August – Meridian, Idaho: Meridian Speedway

26 August – Spokane, Washington: Interstate Fairgrounds Speedway

7 September– Missoula, Montana: Missoula Auto Track

1, 3, 15 September – Salt Lake City, Utah: Utah State Fair

13 October – Carson City, Nevada: Tahoe-Carson Speedway. *Loses control on a jump landing. Breaks hip.*

1969 **24–27 April** – Los Angeles, California: Sports Arena

1970 **23 January** – Daly City, California: Cow Palace
5 April – Kent, Washington: Seattle International Raceway
19 June – Vancouver, British Columbia, Canada: Pacific Coliseum
4 July – Kent, Washington: Seattle International Raceway
16 August – Long Pond, Pennsylvania: Pocono International Raceway
12 December – Los Angeles, California: Lions Drag Strip

1971 **8–9 January** – Houston, Texas: Astrodome
27–28 February – Ontario, California: Ontario Motor Speedway
26–28 March – Chicago, Illinois: Chicago International Amphitheater
10 May – Yakima, Washington; Yakima Speedway. *Breaks collar bone, suffers compound fracture of right arm and breaks both femurs attempting to jump thirteen delivery trucks.*
8–11 July – New York City, New York: Madison Square Garden
15, 17 July – Buffalo, New York: Lancaster Speedway
29–30 July – Wilkes-Barre, Pennsylvania: Pocono Downs
27–28 August – Philadelphia, Pennsylvania: Spectrum
5–6 September – Agawam, Massachusetts: Riverside Park

16–18 September – Great Barrington, Massachusetts: Great Barrington Fair
25–26 September – Hutchinson, Kansas: Kansas State Fair
21 October – Portland, Oregon: Oregon Memorial Coliseum

1972   **23 January** – Tucson, Arizona: Tucson Dragway
11–13 February – Chicago, Illinois: Chicago International Amphitheater
2–3 March – Daly City, California: Cow Palace. *Gets into fight with Hell's Angels in the audience. Jumps successfully, but short landing space means Knievel has to try a sudden stop. He fails, is thrown and is then run over by his own bike. Breaks back and suffers concussion.*
24–26 March – Detroit, Michigan: State Fairgrounds Coliseum
8–9 April – Plymouth, California: Emerson Ranch
11 June – Atlanta, Georgia: Lakewood Speedway
17–18 June – Oklahoma City, Oklahoma: Oklahoma State Fairgrounds
24–25 June – East St Louis, Illinois: St Louis International Raceway
9 July – Haubstadt, Indiana: Tri-State Speedway
16 July – Coon Rapids, Minnesota: Minnesota Dragways
30 July – Castle Rock, Colorado: Continental Divide Raceways
1–2 September – Monroe, Washington: Evergreen Speedway

1973 **5–7 January** – Las Vegas, Nevada: Convention Center
19–21 January – Dallas, Texas: Convention Center
18 February – Los Angeles, California: Memorial Coliseum
23–25 February – Cleveland, Ohio: Convention Center
2–4 March – Uniondale, New York: Nassau Coliseum
16–18 March – Atlanta, Georgia: Lakewood Fairgrounds Exhibit Hall
23–25 March – Chicago, Illinois: Chicago International Amphitheater
30 March –1 April – Detroit, Michigan: State Fairgrounds Coliseum
13–15 April – St Paul, Minnesota: St Paul Civic Center
27–29 April – Cincinnati, Ohio: Cincinnati Gardens
22–24 June – Union Grove, Wisconsin: Great Lakes Dragway
29 July – Providence, Rhode Island: Lincoln Downs Race Track
6–7 October – Kaukauna, Wisconsin: Wisconsin International Raceway
20 October – Philadelphia, Pennsylvania: JFK Stadium

1974 **17 February** – North Richland Hills, Texas: Green Valley Raceway
29 March – Portland, Oregon: Oregon Memorial Coliseum
13 April – Fremont, California: Fremont Raceway
20 April – Irvine, California: Orange County International Raceway
28 April – Kansas City, Missouri: Kansas City International Raceway
5 May – Tulsa, Oklahoma: Tulsa International Speedway

25–27 May – West Salem, Ohio: Dragway 42
20 August – Toronto, Ontario, Canada: Exhibition Stadium
8 September – Twin Falls, Idaho: Snake River Canyon. *Attempts to clear canyon in purpose-built Skycycle – a normal motorcycle with two jet engines capable of producing more than 14,000 pounds' force (62 kN) of thrust bolted onto the sides. Despite both unmanned test jumps in previous years having resulted in the Skycycle's not reaching the other side of the canyon, Knievel goes ahead with the jump. Part way up the take-off ramp, the bike's drogue parachute accidentally opens and the bike fails to reach the other side. As it falls, the main parachute is deployed and the wind carries the bike into the canyon wall. The bike eventually lands half-submerged in the river and Knievel is dragged out, on the same side of the canyon he jumped from, with minor injuries mostly caused by the G-force on take-off.*

1975 **31 May** – London, England: Wembley Stadium. *Attempts to clear thirteen buses. Crashes on landing, breaking pelvis. Is dragged a further twenty yards before the bike lands on top of him, resulting in a broken hand and a compression fracture of a vertebra. Announces retirement over a microphone and walks out of the stadium.*
25 October – Kings Mills, Ohio: Kings Island

1976 **11 October** – Worcester, Massachusetts; Fitton Field
29–30 October – Seattle, Washington: Kingdome

1977 **31 January** – Chicago, Illinois: Chicago International Amphitheater. *During a practice run for a televised special on stuntmen, falls while trying to jump a tank of live sharks.*

*Breaks both arms and collar bone. A cameraman is also
injured and loses an eye.*

1979 **21 February** – Orange, New South Wales, Australia:
Towac Park
23 February – Wollongong, New South Wales,
Australia: Showgrounds
24 February – Sydney, New South Wales, Australia:
RAS Showground
26 February – Wagga Wagga, New South Wales,
Australia: Eric Weissel Oval

1980 **March** – Puerto Rican tour
4 October – Pontiac, Michigan: Silverdome

1981 **31 January–1 February** – St Petersburg, Florida:
Sunshine Speedway
1 March – Hollywood, Florida: Miami-Hollywood
Speedway

1993 *Diagnosed with hepatitis C, contracted as a result of one of his
many blood transfusions.*

1998 **January** – *Falls near a bunker playing golf and has to have a
hip replacement.*
July – *Slips in a Jacuzzi. Breaks rib.*

Index

CPSIA information can be obtained at www.ICGtesting.com
Printed in the USA
LVOW13s1721090214

372970LV00001B/47/P